War Without Consequences

War Without Consequences

Iraq's Insurgency and the Spectre of Strategic Defeat

RUSI Essays 2002–2008

Edited by Terence McNamee

With an Introduction by Sir Jeremy Greenstock

The Royal United Services Institute for Defence and Security Studies

First Published in 2008

Published by RUSI Books
The Royal United Services Institute for Defence and Security Studies (RUSI)
Whitehall London SW1A 2ET United Kingdom

www.rusi.org

© RUSI

All Rights Reserved. No part of this publication may be reproduced, stored in a retrieval system, or transmitted in any form or by any other means, electronic, mechanical, photocopying, recording or otherwise, without prior permission of RUSI.

War Without Consequences: Iraq's Insurgency and the Spectre of Strategic Defeat

ISBN 0-85516-132-9

Printed in Great Britain by Stephen Austin & Sons Ltd.

RUSI is a Registered Charity (No. 210639)

Contents

Foreword   vii

Introduction   ix
Jeremy Greenstock

1. **The 2003 Iraq War – Commander's Reflections**   1
   Brian Burridge

2. **The British Intervention in Iraq: War, Peace and the Costs**   3
   Michael Clarke

3. **The Bush Administration, the War in Iraq and its Consequences for US Policy**   15
   Stephen Fidler

4. **Clarity Through a Dark Glass: Some American Lessons Learned in Iraq**   27
   Thomas Donnelly

5. **Assessing the Surge: A RUSI Interview with Ambassador Ryan Crocker**   39
   October 2007

6. **The US Military After Iraq: A Speculation**   45
   Eliot Cohen
   February 2006

7. **Reforming Iraq's Security Sector**   53
   Andrew Rathmell
   February 2005

8. **Security in Iraq**   61
   Jeremy Greenstock
   October 2004

9. **Military and the Media**   71
   Richard Sambrook
   August 2003

10. **Politics and Governance in the New Iraq: Reconstruction**   83
    of the New Versus Resurrection of the Old
    Gareth Stansfield
    May 2003

11. **Europe and the United States: An End to Illusions**   105
    Jonathan Eyal
    May 2003

12. **Between Peace and War: Iraq in Perspective**   123
    Douglas Hurd
    February 2003

13. **High Noon for British Grand Strategy**   127
    Michael Codner
    October 2002

End Note   139
   Ghost Stories
   John Nagl
   December 2007

Foreword

About one month after President Bush delivered his 'Mission Accomplished' speech from the deck of the USS *Abraham Lincoln*, RUSI published a *Whitehall Paper* entitled 'The Iraq War – Combat and Consequence'. Then, as now, the 'combat' was described as a triumph of Coalition firepower and strategy. Speculation on the 'consequence', however, ranged widely. It was June 2003 and Iraq was chaotic and traumatised. But from the outside you could have been forgiven for thinking the worst was over.

Five years on from the 'end' of the war, its consequences are all too evident – in the countless victims of the insurgency, the diminished global reputation of America (and to a lesser extent, Britain), the emergence of Al-Qa'ida in Iraq, an emboldened Iran and the colossal financial toll of occupation. And yet, as Sir Jeremy Greenstock reminds us in his introduction to this book, we still do not know how it is going to turn out. The success of the 'surge' hints at the possibility of outcomes other than state failure and recurring cycles of violence.

Whatever the future holds for Iraq, it is now an article of faith on both sides of the Atlantic that in the planning and preparation for the war due consideration was not given – at least by those who called the shots – to the forces that could be unleashed in its aftermath.

War Without Consequences is a collection of new writing and previously published essays examining the conflict in Iraq. A brief reflection on the war by the commander of the UK invasion force, Sir Brian Burridge, is followed by an analysis of its strategic implications for the UK armed forces and British defence policy by the Director of RUSI, Michael Clarke. The next two essays feature contrasting perspectives on the war's impact on the US military and America's foreign policy. The defence and security editor of the *Financial Times*, Stephen Fidler, argues that because of the war America is 'less feared' and 'less loved' than it was in 2003, the year historians might one day cite as the high water mark of American power. Thomas Donnelly of the American Enterprise Institute is far more sanguine. He explores how, through bitter experience, the military that invaded Iraq has transformed itself into a remarkably agile and innovative counter-insurgency force. If sustained, the success of the surge may, Donnelly suggests, reinvigorate America's commitment to its wider,

Long War project.

Six months before the invasion, RUSI's Michael Codner warned in an article published in the *RUSI Journal* that 'we cannot assume Iraqi people anywhere will see the forces of an invading and occupying coalition as liberators.' Five years and numerous 'lessons learned' analyses later, we published a cautiously optimistic assessment by the US Ambassador to Iraq, Ryan Crocker. Both articles plus other essays originally published in the *Whitehall Paper* and in the *RUSI Journal* since October 2002 feature in the remainder of this book.

Dr Terence McNamee
Royal United Services Institute
Whitehall, London
March 2008

Introduction

Jeremy Greenstock

Five years on from the invasion of Iraq, we still do not know how it is all going to turn out. Hindsight makes it progressively easier to criticise the Coalition, and particularly the United States, for their woefully inadequate planning and their bad mismatch of resources to tasks after the conflict was over. We cannot just put these mistakes behind us and move on, because the consequences have seriously affected, at least for a while, the credibility of the US and the UK in the international arena, the range of instruments they can legitimately and effectively bring to bear in the Middle East and their capacity to give due priority to other pressing problems. Both Iran and Afghanistan, for instance, are current challenges whose handling could benefit from the lessons of Iraq.

Nonetheless time is needed to show where the people of Iraq in the end manage to take their hard-won yet dangerous opportunity. In a number of other troubled regions of the world, the greater freedom of choice generated by new millennium developments has led to schism rather than cohesion. While continued violence is inevitable in Iraq for some years yet, there are possible outcomes other than unmitigated disaster. For that reason, and because a vacuum can create fresh dangers, it remains my view that Coalition troops need to stay for quite some time into the future, provided they are not asked to leave by the sovereign Iraqi government.

Even within this five-year period, it has taken a long time for lessons to be absorbed from the early setbacks. Fifth Anniversary retrospectives will cover in some detail the things that were done and the things that should have been done. This volume by RUSI assembles essays from 2002 to the present on aspects ranging from pre-war concerns over the role of occupying forces and the impact on transatlantic relations to the traumatic resurrection of sectarian violence in the war's aftermath and Washington's change of strategy to tackle the insurgency.

The tragedy is that a large number of players on the ground, in small groups or individually, acted courageously and resourcefully to try to achieve what the governments in Washington and London wanted: they included army officers in their theatre of operations, civilian affairs officers alongside them, political appointees in the provinces, planners and advisers in Baghdad. Lives were risked and occasionally lost in putting the interests of the Iraqi people first or in trying to sort out local problems. From these experiences came valuable adjustments, which have fed into some of the improvements seen from the second half of 2007 onwards. General David Petraeus, the architect of many of the operational advances made in this recent period, would not have known how to secure these better results without the searing experience of his tour of duty in the North-West of Iraq, when – as far as I could see from the relative distance of Baghdad – he followed his own instincts more consistently than his tactical instructions from higher up the line. Yet they were all let down by a high-level failure to provide a strategic framework combining understanding of the complexity of the task, knowledge of the terrain and deployment of adequate resources. Thomas Ricks's book *Fiasco* sets out as graphically as any I have read the gap between haphazard strategy at the centre and ingenious effort at the capillaries.

Nothing was so careless as the approach to security in theatre. It all started to go wrong immediately after the conflict was over on 9 April 2003. After a meticulously planned and executed invasion, the light-switch was turned off. I have never really been able to understand how General Tommy Franks, CENTCOM Commander and the military architect of Saddam's downfall, was allowed to assume that his job was done when Baghdad collapsed. He never gave, and was never asked to give, the same priority to the fourth phase of the operation, the handling of Iraq after victory, as to the first three. Where was the continuity? Franks ought to have been instructed, preferably in mid-2002, to produce a secure Iraq beyond Saddam and to stay at least six months into the post-conflict period. Instead, assumptions were made about the capacity of Iraqi society to re-form itself in an ordered way which did not stand up against the historical evidence or the expectations of those who knew Iraq well. No insurance policy was drawn up. The momentum of American deployed power was judged to be enough. From then on it was all about shocked reactions to unexpected outcomes – as in the transfer of civilian authority from Jay Garner to Paul Bremer – or about straight denial. No-one given authority on the ground in Iraq in this period, including myself, was big enough to overcome these fundamental disadvantages of strategy, structure and resources.

Introduction

Would the attack on Iraq have led to a different outcome if the planning and the strategy had been solid? Who can tell? I believed at the time it was possible and I still do, but that is to put faith in the emergence of a responsible and effective political leadership in Baghdad which is not yet visible. The considerable talents of the Iraqi people may, over the next generation, find a way to come to terms with their fissiparous nature, their violent history and the grievous volumes of blood spilt. They may be able to create the compromises necessary for a united country to survive. But what a cost in time, lives and money! Years of potential progress were sacrificed in those first few days in April and the damage will be felt far beyond Iraq for a long while to come.

This selection of commentaries is therefore important reading not just to understand what went wrong, but because there are still decisions to be made and outcomes to be fought for. From a range of possible policies to be pursued, above all in Washington, there is not a single one that will avoid pain. But we cannot walk away from this country if its government continues to want our input. General Ricardo Sanchez, the Coalition's Commanding officer in Baghdad from June 2003–June 2004, often used to say that US forces could not be strategically defeated in Iraq. That was true in terms of military strength on the ground. But one of the enduring lessons of Iraq will be that the conventional military calculations of the twentieth century have lost their relevance in the twenty-first century's accelerating redeployment of effective power. Strategic defeat can come in other forms; and the context and the instruments have changed for good. We have to assess where that leaves us for the real life battles ahead.

Sir Jeremy Greenstock was the United Kingdom's Ambassador to the United Nations at the time of the US-led invasion in March 2003. From September 2003 to March 2004 he served as the UK Special Representative to Iraq. He is currently Director of the Ditchley Foundation.

1. The 2003 Iraq War – Commander's Reflections

Brian Burridge

Air Chief Marshal Sir Brian Burridge commanded the UK Joint contingent of 43,000 personnel in the 2003 Iraq War. He spent thirty-nine years as a pilot in the Royal Air Force. He has held a front-line command at every level in the Service and spent a number of years in the Ministry of Defence in policy posts, including almost three years as the Principal Staff Officer to the Chief of the Defence Staff. He left the Royal Air Force in January 2006 as Commander-in-Chief Strike Command and is now Vice President Strategic Marketing for Finmeccanica UK.

> *'I shall proceed from the simple to the complex. But in war more than in any other subject we must begin by looking at the nature of the whole; for here more than elsewhere the part and the whole must always be thought of together.'*
>
> *Clausewitz*

In reflecting on the events of five years ago, I often return to this wisdom from Clausewitz. In so doing, I am often struck by the ease with which the significance of events becomes clouded as commentators seek to re-engineer history. First, it is after all a fact that, on 18 March 2003 after nine hours of debate, the House of Commons voted by a majority of 203 to send UK forces into Iraq. I well remember watching the proceedings from my command post in Qatar, wondering how I would explain a defeat of the Government to my US counterpart. The preceding Sunday's anti-war demonstration in London of almost a million people, with shades of Suez about it, had already given us all food for thought. But it is also a fact that the intelligence on Iraq's real capability and, more importantly, Saddam's real intentions was dubious. Hence, the debate itself took place on a shaky premise. And I remember, too, the uneasy feeling developing in my mind as site after site yielded no WMD as the Iraq Survey Group moved through the country. Secondly, it is also a fact that the US State Department had spent many months leading a talented task force planning for the aftermath of an invasion of Iraq. Yet, it is another fact that, when responsibility for Phase IV was passed to the Pentagon, the resulting plans plus the clever and experienced minds that underpinned them were consigned to the waste bin. To discover that the Office of Reconstruction and Humanitarian Assistance did not, after all, have access to thousands of US contractors at high readiness on which immediate reconstruction would depend was deeply unsettling. Thirdly, it is a fact that dissolving the Iraqi Army, de-Ba'athification of public institutions and the rejection of quickly placing governance, however imperfect, in the hands of Iraqis led to chaos in the early months. And I remember the disbelief that we felt in the UK headquarters that anyone could ride so roughshod over the lessons of history. Aldous Huxley was right when he said, 'that men do not learn very much from the lessons of history is the most important of all the lessons that history has to teach'.

So have we learned the lessons of our recent history? Certainly, I judge that we are on track for a War Powers Act and that decision-makers will be much more circumspect over their use of intelligence in the years to come. As for aftermath planning following military intervention, there is little tangible evidence that the much vaunted, pan-Whitehall Comprehensive Approach has gained real traction: it simply must achieve proper momentum if history is not to repeat itself. But many of the military lessons were positive and enduring. The delegation of targeting authority to commanders in theatre was well conducted, greatly easing the problems of maintaining momentum and staying in step with the US. The Royal Navy's Tomahawks proved very flexible in achieving effect across the spectrum of conflict. Although our grasp of land/air integration and post-attack assessment capability were less than perfect, the sheer effectiveness of the current generation of precision-guided weapons, not least Storm Shadow, made the debacle of the 1999 Kosovo air campaign seem a distant memory. But the most compelling lesson for me was that the 'British Way of Warfare' – mission command, manoeuvre warfare and decisive effect – is absolutely the right doctrine. And the most compelling memory was undoubtedly the sheer determination, courage and grit displayed by some very young and junior soldiers in situations where they were required to display levels of professionalism, leadership and flexibility that is a great tribute to the British Army's training process and to the strength of the Regimental system. Clausewitz would certainly have approved.

2. The British Intervention in Iraq
War, Peace and the Costs

Michael Clarke

Professor Michael Clarke is the Director of RUSI.

The second Iraq war was a controversial conflict from its inception. Five years on from the end of formal hostilities, it is difficult to see it as anything other than a strategic blunder. Whether this will remain a valid judgement in another five or ten years will depend upon much larger events in the Middle East and elsewhere. A functioning and unified Iraq within a region where stability and prosperity grows through deepening Western influence is certainly possible to imagine, but that trajectory is not evident at the moment. For now, the overall judgement on the US-led war must be that it was a blunder, in the sense that the major powers that prosecuted it would have been better if they had not acted at all. If their objectives were to prevent another nuclear power arising in the region, to deprive Iraq of chemical or biological weapons, to prevent the dissemination of jihadist terror against Western countries, or to prevent a dictator's destabilising influence within the region (containment having been deemed to fail), then doing nothing would have left the Western powers in a better position than they now find themselves.

The power that has emerged with the greatest strategic gain from the war up to this point is unquestionably Iran. The influence of Tehran around the region grows in ways that are clearly antithetical to Western policy. Iran seems determined to give itself the capacity to exercise a nuclear weapons option. Turkey, Egypt, and the states of the Gulf Cooperation Council are all accelerating embryonic nuclear programmes as a hedge against that eventuality.

The grand strategic bargain in the approach to war that attempted to create a unified Western front against Iraq, legitimised through the UN, tied to a reinvigorated 'road map' for an Israeli-Palestinian peace deal, and set within the context of growing democratisation throughout the region, was as tenuous as it was ambitious.[1] Save for the removal of a vicious dictator in itself – a matter of no small importance to Iraqis whatever their present miseries – the war has so far achieved none of the international strategic objectives that were claimed for it. The position of Washington and its allies in the Middle East is clearly worse in 2008 than it was in 2003, in terms of the imminence of nuclear proliferation, the stimulus to global terrorism, regional stability, Western diplomatic strength in the region or influence over Middle Eastern energy supplies. While there has been some good news on the military and security front in the last year, as the change of tactics and political alignments surrounding the US 'troop surge' has borne fruit, the fact remains that, at best, such gains take the coalition back to the position it expected to be in around the end of 2003. And a legacy from the last five years is unavoidable.

If this somewhat depressing judgement must be applied to the enterprise as a whole, the question arises as to what this means for the UK as Washington's most loyal ally. How are we to understand the strategic impact on the UK of an enterprise not of our own making, but one to which the commitment was instinctive, politically expensive, and in the longer-term perspective on transatlantic relations, probably the right thing to do – blunder or not? In this respect, history may be kinder to Tony Blair than his contemporaries have been. It would have been unthinkable for the UK not to support the United States over Iraq after all that had gone before. What is at issue is rather the manner and extent of support, given such a poorly executed US policy and the price the UK has paid for it. In the end, Tony Blair argued in Parliament for the war simply because it was morally right to remove a brutal dictator. This was not a strategic argument and can only be assessed in the conscience of the nation. The strategic implications of the war for the UK are a matter of more equivocal calculations.

Two Different Wars

At both the operational and strategic levels, the British and the Americans have been fighting significantly different wars in Iraq for much of the last five years. The two major allies crossed the start line together on 20 March 2003 and then went north and east respectively, getting further away from each other and fighting their own type of conventional ground war (to 'kick the door in') followed by their own type of counter-insurgency operation (to 'win hearts and minds') in two separate Iraqi environments which posed different challenges for them both. Their wars have been different, too, on their own domestic and political fronts.

At the operational level, UK forces faced a significantly different environment in the four southern provinces and the city of Basra under their control. Predominantly Shia and with the commercial and oil wealth that gave Basra an identity of its own, UK forces were able to operate in a more relaxed fashion during the first year after the war, concentrating on reconstruction tasks, building support among local leaders and supporting a political resurrection of traditional tribal authority. Iranian influence was also naturally high in the southern provinces where the border between Iraq and Iran was highly porous. Smuggling and organised criminality was, and remains, extensive. UK forces did not try to take this on directly. Their operations were designed to work with the grain of what they found on the ground. With this characteristically 'softer' British approach, in contrast to that of US forces further north, UK forces were able to deal easily with the first uprising of the so-called Mahdi Army in the spring of 2004. It was snuffed out in Basra with the judicious use of limited force and political pressure through local leaders. The British were able to exploit the opportunities provided by an essentially favourable environment and the progress they made was held up by many observers as an example of superior tactics in such delicate post-war operations. However, the situation gradually changed.

The killing of six British military police by a mob in Maja Al-Kabir in 2003 might have served as a warning of events to come, but the area around Al-Amara in the north of Britain's Multi-National Division South East (MND(SE)) was regarded as a separate problem and not typical of the region as a whole. Nevertheless, throughout 2004 and 2005 the security situation in and around Basra, though not in most of the remainder of MND(SE), deteriorated as a reflection of events further north in Baghdad. The accelerating Mahdi Army uprising, local disorder and growing resentment across the country at coalition forces that now appeared as an occupying force eventually spilled into the UK's area of operations. The inability to restore enough robust infrastructure and deliver economic development to Basra and its hinterland only fed the unrest.

Though objectives of British forces did not change, there were inevitable tactical shifts. The deployment in late 2004 of the Snatch Land Rover, a legacy from Northern Ireland, symbolised a significant recognition of the more dangerous operational environment, as did the deployment of the Black Watch battalion to Camp Dogwood at the end of 2004 as part of the decisive US push to recapture Fallujah. By 2005, British troops had been forced back into their armoured vehicles. The scope for useful military action in MND(SE) was narrowing rather than widening; an interesting contrast with previous military operations in Bosnia, Kosovo or Sierra Leone. A step-change took place at the end of 2006 when Operation *Blenheim* – renamed and extended as Operation *Sinbad* – aimed to create a decisive push to re-establish governmental authority and attack the worst of police corruption in and around Basra. It was a muscular military response to the fact that UK forces had few remaining options but to hand over to Iraqi security forces in as good order as possible. *Sinbad*, however, was operationally successful and created a momentum that was extended by the local Iraqi authorities themselves. Muthanna province had been handed over to Iraqi control in July 2006, Dhi Qar in September. Maysan province was transferred in April 2007 and finally in December 2007, Basra was handed to local forces while UK troops withdrew to Basra air station to remove them from Basra city itself.

This story of Operation *Telic* is subject to very different interpretations. The official view is that the job has now largely been done, save for the residual roles of providing some continuing assistance to the Iraqi authorities and acting, if necessary, as a strategic reserve. The present commitment – Operation *Overwatch* – will continue at some sustainable level between perhaps 2,500 and 4,200 troops, plus the backup from Royal Navy and RAF operations. This might be maintained for some time depending on broader political conditions. The most negative view of Operation *Telic* is that it has been characterised first by hubris – in assuming that the British just 'did' peace-building inherently better than the Americans; then by denial – in refusing to address the real causes of instability in MND(SE); and finally by delusion – in masking an effective retreat as an ordered hand-over to Iraqi authorities. Certainly, thinkers from the left in Britain and from the right in the United States have both taken versions of this view.[2]

A more accurate interpretation of the operational record of UK forces, however, certainly recognises that the deteriorating security situation hustled the British into more of a counter-insurgency role as opposed to the peace-building operations they began with, and forced them into more militarised responses than they had anticipated. From the perspective of post-conflict reconstruction, the fact that the best way to reduce violence in Basra was eventually to withdraw from it, is very telling. The question, 'At what point did we lose Basra?' is a legitimate one. Nevertheless, even in this unfavourable situation the British operation succeeded in two important respects. Firstly, the timetable for creating democratic institutions in Iraq was met and throughout 2005 and the first half of 2006 Basra and the other provinces in MND(SE) took a full part in the creation of a National Assembly, the referendum on a constitution, and the creation of a national government in Baghdad. Crucial provincial elections must still take place, having been repeatedly put off to diffuse the tension they will inevitably generate throughout the country. This is indicative. Though Iraq's new democratic institutions have not had a decisive effect on the security equation or on social cohesion and have so far proved weak and disappointing, the fact remains that their existence is an essential pre-requisite to any stable future for the country.

Secondly, UK forces have demonstrably succeeded in training over 20,000 Iraqi troops and largely creating two new Iraqi National Army divisions to keep order in the sector. The 10th Division, now operating mainly in the surrounding provinces, and the 14th Division in Basra city are fully operational and well-led, at least from the top. Questions may remain as to how well they will perform under stress, and training is now concentrating on technical specialisms and the personal quality of the officers and NCOs in their ranks. But to date, both of these formations have done all that has been asked of them and levels of violence in the MND(SE) area are currently low. Far less has been achieved with the Iraq Police Service despite some £133 million spent by the UK in training efforts over the last five years. Overall, however, it is evident that UK forces have managed to shepherd into being a viable political and security apparatus to whom it could hand over, albeit in something of a scramble. The robustness of those arrangements is yet to be tested and economic reconstruction and development in Basra is still barely acceptable five years on. But the UK has almost reached what might be regarded as its de facto fallback position in this venture: that whatever happens in the south of Iraq may soon be fairly regarded as the responsibility of the Iraqis themselves, not the invaders of 2003.

This is not an operational position in which US forces currently find themselves.[3] There is a clear difference between the two allies in this respect and the reasons are to be found at the strategic level. It is not too much to say that beyond the removal of Saddam Hussein, the UK and the United States appear to have had little genuinely common purpose. Whatever Tony Blair personally felt about the rationale for the operation, it was not in the nature of Britain's defence and foreign policy establishment to commit itself to a long-term democratisation project in the heart of the Middle East. For Britain, a minimal level of post-war stability in Iraq was good enough. No matter that southern Iraq was characteristically lawless and resentful of Baghdad. We would not try to change it. No matter that Iranian influence was naturally high in the south. We would use it as a potential diplomatic opening to Tehran to discuss common interests in Iraq and a wider range of strategic issues with Iranian leaders. Attempts to do just this were a persistent source of irritation to US observers, many of whom felt that the whole UK approach was not just too permissive but lacking in strategic coherence. The truth was rather that the UK had very little genuine input to the strategy and only limited influence over the Iraqi political environment within which it was trying to work.

Once it became clear that coalition forces were not welcomed into Iraq as liberators within a society ready to bounce back quickly from the effects of war – the fundamental assumption of US planning for the operation – the coalition's strategy for the future was being made up as it went along. The complete lack of planning for post-war reconstruction in 'Phase IV' of the operational design threw all in the coalition back on their instincts. And their instincts flowed as much as anything else from their tactics.[4] But it was not only that the central reconstruction strategy was at first lacking, and then when it existed, lacking in implementation: applying it within the Coalition Provisional Authority somehow made no impact outside Baghdad's 'green zone'.

This, in itself, led to the elevation of tactics over strategy. The Iraqi Government itself did not produce even an outline national security strategy until the middle of 2007.[5] For the British there was also the problem that they were essentially at the mercy of the political ebb and flow around Baghdad and within the 'Sunni triangle'. Though the Shia south was not part of the Sunni-led insurgency which quickly became part of an Al-Qa'ida offensive, the different insurgencies overlapped each other and easily fed wider sectarian, local and criminal violence over which the British had no political influence at the national level.

Other peace-building and counter-insurgency operations the British have successfully conducted, from Malaya to Northern Ireland, to Bosnia or Sierra Leone, have been based on the pre-requisite that the military and political levels of activity have to be conducted vigorously, and in close co-ordination. British authorities, in effect, 'owned' most of the political space they were operating in during these missions. This was never possible at the national level in Iraq, for reasons that have been well-recorded elsewhere, and it was only possible at the local level in the south once the Iraqi administrations in Baghdad were prepared to place tough bureaucrats in the region with a brief to co-operate fully with the military. This did not happen until well into 2005, too late to prevent the narrowing of useful military options. Unless the UK was prepared to commit considerably more forces to Operation *Telic* to try to reverse local trends – and there was no political appetite for that – the lack of sufficient political control at local levels made the eventual timetable for a hasty handover more or less inevitable.

The Judgement of Costs and Strategy

The total financial cost of the British operation in Iraq, including some £850 million spent in the conflict itself, has been in the order of £7 billion over the last five years. The current cost in 2007-08 has jumped by over 50 per cent on the previous year's calculations to £1.4 billion.[6] This is not indicative of a big rise in real costs as the operation has wound down, rather an admission on the part of the Ministry of Defence (MoD) that previous estimates had omitted too many relevant items and that operations such as this are inherently difficult to cost accurately. The absolute numbers involved in this gross costing are high, but hardly unsustainable at the national level. The costs of wars are met from the Treasury's contingency reserve, but those of 'normal' operations and commitments are part of the defence budget, currently set at £32.6 billion. Clearly, the distinction between 'war' and 'normality' is an inherently political calculation and will eventually affect any defence budget that is not growing in real terms. The MoD is enduring a tough spending round in any case and the current costs of Iraq can only add to the pressure. An annual cost for

Iraq running at around £1.4 billion puts a different perspective on the proposed £3 billion cuts in the equipment budget that is currently absorbing so much of the MoD's energy.

The real effect of Iraq costs is not that the country cannot afford them, but that (along with comparable costs for current Afghanistan operations) they narrow all the options in the defence budget for dealing with other priorities, however much is taken from the contingency reserve in a given year. Equipment uses up its operational life more quickly, replacements have to be brought forward earlier, urgent operational requirements have to be placed regularly to cope with necessary tactical shifts and the technical enablers in all operations – communications, intelligence, engineering, and so on – become expensively stretched.

There are less tangible costs to the Armed Forces themselves from Iraqi operations, which play into the national calculation of costs and benefits. Iraq has cost the lives of 175 service personnel to date and there are over 800 with serious wounds and disability. The psychological impact of these losses is driven by the perception of the operation. If the operation is seen as less than vital, not connected directly enough to British interests; if we perceive we are near the end of the whole engagement, or that losses are caused somehow by random enemy action; then figures such as these loom very large in the public and political mind. And while members of volunteer armed forces will always accept that they take their chances in the profession they have chosen, losses will have an impact on their own morale in the same way. Infantry units in Iraq and Afghanistan together have suffered losses of up to 11 per cent – a Second World War casualty rate. That may be sustainable in conditions of national mobilisation, but it stretches the fabric when a society considers itself to be in a time of peace. Further, the moral lapses in behaviour among all the forces in Iraq have created iconic images of abuse and excess. The rough justice that soldiers have traditionally meted out extra-judicially and the quite exceptional chaos exhibited at the Abu Ghraib prison in Baghdad in 2003, have become lodged in the public's consciousness and resulted in a corrosive scepticism over the justification for the operation.

By 2005, the Guardian/ICM's regular polling within the UK reported that 51 per cent of the public favoured a withdrawal of British troops within a year. By October 2006, this had grown to 61 per cent and has remained around that level since – including a core of around 45 per cent of respondents who say they favour immediate withdrawal regardless.[7] This is consistent with international attitudes measured by Globescan for the BBC which reports 67 per cent of respondents in twenty-two countries in favour of an immediate US withdrawal (and hence an abrupt ending of the whole operation), not to mention almost 50 per cent who assume, nevertheless, that the US will stay in Iraq indefinitely for its own strategic reasons.[8]

The broader strategic costs to the UK, of what has been defined here as a blunder, may be surprisingly equivocal. Blunders, like successes, are replete with unintended consequences. The UK being prepared to pay so high a price to stand with the US and the presumption within government that British forces will not finally withdraw from the operation until the Americans do are important elements in the UK's long-term international positioning. The sense that 'We went in together, we will come out together' persists. How much direct influence this buys the UK in Washington is much debated. But the argument should not be about direct influence with an outgoing Bush presidency, so much as the investment it represents in the UK taking an international position alongside the United States for a coming generation of politicians. Germany and France have worked hard under new leaderships to get back on terms with the US after the alliance crisis of 2003, while the Brown government has distanced itself from the present White House, and in turn has been distanced by it. It is not a zero-sum diplomatic game, however, and Britain's positioning in the way that Tony Blair envisioned it is intended to transcend immediate interests to help elevate the 'anglosphere' countries to moral and political leadership in a world where democratic forces are now under pressure and where liberal-capitalist progress can no longer be taken for granted. As a matter of strategic positioning, this may have something to recommend it.[9] But since the object of the positioning has centred on the Iraq project, even under its existing UN mandate, it clearly runs counter to current trends in domestic and international public opinion. A perception of longer-term success in Iraq – say over the coming decade – would greatly strengthen the force of this stance. Conversely, any sense that Iraq was fracturing irrevocably would make it appear quite hollow.

In the more immediate future, other contradictory trends are evident. On the one hand, Britain's own status in the Middle East has undoubtedly suffered from the Iraq war and there is some bewilderment in Arab capitals as to why Britain has been so committed. Arguments about 'positioning' and moral leadership do not find ready understanding in such places. There is, too, a current sense of exasperation that Gordon Brown and his key ministers seem to have given scant attention to Middle East affairs during their first year. The leadership's concentration on South and East Asia has been repeatedly noted in Arab capitals and embassies around the world. On the other hand, the fact that Britain is now so deeply enmeshed in the future of Iraq and of Western policy towards Iran, even against a better judgement, gives it some influence in the region. Since Britain has invested so much in the current relationship with the Bush Administration, it remains one of the diplomatic transmission mechanisms to Washington. London is still regarded as having direct input to US policy on not only Iraq, but also on other issues. If a meaningful Israeli-Palestinian peace process begins again sometime in the next two years, and that can only happen if the US makes it come about, many Arab capitals assume that Britain will be an influential player in it.

If, paradoxically, there may be something to hope for in the Middle East, on the European front the future of Iraq has been a damaging distraction with few compensatory possibilities. The strategic task for Britain and its other European partners has become nothing less than to save NATO and make something militarily capable out of the sclerotic state of most individual European defence inventories. Then, it is to link European collective military capacities to the civilianised 'soft power' potential of a European Union that encompasses 490 million people and accounts for 25 per cent of global GDP. This is a big strategic undertaking by any standards. The articulation of America's War on Terror from the beginning of 2002, the approach to war, and the five years of aftermath in Iraq put all of this on the UK's back-burner. What progress has been made among the European allies on this undertaking has generally not been driven by the UK, within either NATO or the European Union. The assertive Franco-British leadership that promised much at the St Malo summit in 1998 ran aground on the antagonism between Blair and Chirac over Iraq and it has not so far been replicated by any Brown-Sarkozy axis. Instead, the focus has shifted to Afghanistan where NATO's relevance as a global organisation and its competence as a collective alliance is being severely tested.

UK defence planners in early 2005, when NATO made its commitment to Afghanistan, hoped that Britain's contribution (now at 7,700 troops) could be accommodated by a drawdown in Iraq. This became one of the implicit drivers of the Iraqi handover timetable from 2005. Both the Iraq and Afghanistan commitments, however, are likely to remain at a level that exceeds initial expectations. This puts particular strain on key force enablers, logistics and reserves. It is difficult to see how UK forces can 'run hot' in this way indefinitely.[10] Nevertheless, NATO's success in Afghanistan is now probably more important to Britain's overall strategic position in the next decade than the future of Iraq, critical though that is. For a collapse in NATO's credibility as a working alliance would have severe consequences for the transatlantic relationship as a whole, on the future of European security through the EU and indeed on the implicit security equation that has kept Europe free and prosperous in a manner that has cost the UK very little to help sustain. Current levels of security and reassurance in Europe would be far more difficult and expensive if they had to be viewed through a series of national, rather than an essentially collective, lenses – and without an institutional link to the United States. For the sake of its broader transatlantic and European interests, therefore, Britain somehow has to balance two difficult military and political commitments, one which fundamentally affects its bilateral relationship with the US and its leverage in the Middle East; the other which fundamentally affects its alliance relationship with the US and with all of its significant European partners. Perceived failure in either or both of these arenas over the coming years would seriously undermine the foundations on which UK security has been built since the late 1940s.

It is, of course, too late to go back on our Iraqi policy and do it differently. The Armed Forces may logically now have achieved more or less all they usefully can in the shifting and unfavourable circumstances in southern Iraq. But the political battle still to draw some strategic success out of the Iraqi blunder cannot be dodged; not from a moral point of view and certainly not in terms of what is now in the UK's long-term strategic interests.

Notes

[1] Philip H Gordon and Jeremy Shapiro, *Allies at war: America, Europe and the crisis over Iraq* (New York: McGraw-Hill, 2004).

² Summary of views in Karen De Young and Thomas E. Ricks, 'As Britain leaves, Basra deteriorates', *Washington Post*, 7 August 2007, p. A01: Richard Beeston, 'Britain on the way out', *New Statesman*, 6 September 2007.

³ See, for example, Olga Oliker et al, *US policy options for Iraq: a reassessment* (Santa Monica, CA: Rand Corporation, 2007).

⁴ Thomas E Ricks, *Fiasco: The American military adventure in Iraq* (London: Penguin Books, 2007), pp. 206-13.

⁵ National Security Advisor, Federal Government of Iraq, *Iraq First: The Iraqi National Security Strategy 2007-2010*, 2007.

⁶ See: House of Commons Defence Committee, 2005, *Continuing operations in Iraq* (London: The Stationery Office), para. 149; Ministry of Defence, *Operations in Iraq: lessons for the future* (London: The Stationery Office, 2004), p. 70-71; House of Commons Defence Committee, *Operational costs in Afghanistan and Iraq: spring supplementary estimates 2007-08*, HC 400 (London: The Stationery Office, 2008), para.10.

⁷ Guardian/ICM poll, reported as, 'Iraq: voters want British troops home by end of year', *The Guardian*, 24 October 2006, p.1.

⁸ BBC/Globescan poll. BBC World Service, 6 September 2007.

⁹ On Blair's sense of positioning, see, Michael Clarke, 'Foreign policy', in Anthony Seldon (ed.), *Blair's Britain, 1997-2007* (Cambridge: Cambridge University Press, 2007), pp. 597-603. On the influence and potential of the 'anglosphere' see Walter Russell Mead, *God and gold: Britain, America and the making of the modern world* (London: Atlantic Books, 2007).

¹⁰ Comments made by General Sir Richard Dannatt as Chief of the General Staff: 'Straight talking and more to come' *The Guardian*, 14 October 2006, p. 3.

3. The Bush Administration, the War in Iraq and its Consequences for US Policy

Stephen Fidler

Stephen Fidler is the Defence and Security Editor of the *Financial Times*. Based in Washington from 1998 to the end of 2001, he was reassigned there temporarily in early 2003 to cover the invasion.

If the success of a war is measured by its achievements set against its cost, then the military campaign that started with the US-led invasion of Iraq in 2003 appears, five years on, to have been one of the most spectacularly unsuccessful of all time.

It is, of course, as Zhou Enlai might have said, too early to judge what might be the war's final achievements. But we already know that many of the benefits that Washington cited for the invasion have not accrued.

Perhaps the most advertised justification for the war was to rid Iraq of weapons of mass destruction. But Iraq possessed none, save a few rusting containers of chemical agent. Another supposed benefit was to derive from breaking an alleged nexus between Saddam Hussein and Osama bin Laden's Al-Qa'ida network. Yet it is now almost certain that no such links of any importance existed: Iraq in 2003, unlike today, was one Middle Eastern state where the terrorist organisation had few, if any, adherents. Indeed, the Iraq war may have resulted in a severe reversal of the struggle against terrorism because of its role in fuelling radicalisation across the globe and in depriving resources, financial and otherwise, from the broader campaign. A further reason cited as a justification was to stop the human rights abuses by Saddam Hussein's regime. But while the Baghdad government no longer presides over a Republic of Fear, this has come with a heavy human cost: the violence and chaos that followed the invasion have taken, by conservative estimates, more than a hundred thousand lives.

Some of the war's supporters also expressed the hope that the Middle East could be remade – and the path to Israeli-Palestinian peace eased – if the dictatorship in Baghdad was replaced by a democratic government. Yet, there is no sign yet of any resolution of the Israeli-

Palestinian conflict. And if indeed the Middle East has been remade at all, it looks, five years on, as if this could be inimical to American interests. Indeed, America's greatest strategic adversary in the region, Iran, appears to have been emboldened by the US political and military obsession with Iraq. Furthermore, if the war was part of an effort to demonstrate the efficacy of American hard power to the world, it appears to have done the opposite. Finally, if the war was at any level 'about oil' – and presumably the US preoccupation with Iraq had something to do with that commodity – then Iraqi crude oil output has struggled to reach pre-invasion levels, even as the oil price has trebled.

If the benefits remain modest and uncertain, the costs are more evident, if still growing. Calculations by the Nobel Prize winning economist Joseph Stiglitz and the Harvard University public finance specialist Linda Bilmes suggest the war's cost to the *United States* will be $3 trillion, more than of any war in US history, except for the Second World War, whose benefits were rather more tangible. This includes $845 billion of direct operational costs that will have been voted by Congress until the end of fiscal year 2008 (which also includes funds for Afghanistan); hidden costs buried in the defence budget, including equipment that is estimated to be wearing out at six to ten times the peacetime rate; the costs of borrowing to finance the war; and the costs of death and disability benefits for the 4,000 killed and 60,000 US soldiers injured in the conflict. In this latter respect, they noted that benefits paid out to Second World War veterans peaked in 1993. Other serious estimates suggest the costs will run well into the trillions of dollars. Given that the highest pre-war estimate was $100-200 billion – from the White national economic advisor, Lawrence Lindsey, who was dismissed for his frankness soon after – the miscalculation, when measured in financial terms alone, was extraordinary. And the estimates ignore the costs borne outside the United States, which may approach a similar enormous figure.

This miscalculation will, of course, weigh heavily on the legacy of George W. Bush. To the extent that the blood and treasure expended on Iraq constrains the freedom of US actions, military and otherwise, the responsibility must lie at his door. Indeed, for the 'virtual historian', it is fascinating to ponder how different would have been the first decade of the twenty-first century if a few hundred more Floridians, or one more Supreme Court justice, had voted for Al Gore in the 2000 US presidential election. The attacks of 11 September 2001, assuming they were not thwarted, would inevitably have framed a Gore presidency, just as they did in fact for George W. Bush's. But it is hard to imagine that barely eighteen months later Gore would have embarked on an invasion of a country that, in spite of the ugliness of its government, was scarcely linked, if at all, to the atrocity.

But even Bush might not have gone to war in Iraq if he had surrounded himself with different people. One fateful decision was his appointment of Dick Cheney as his running mate after Cheney, appointed to head the committee to search for Bush's deputy, failed to find another candidate whom he deemed suitable. Cheney brought into the administration people of similar stripe, constructing a national security executive along Cold War lines that seemed to find its post facto justification in 9/11. Most notably, he recruited Donald Rumsfeld as defence secretary, the pair combining to become a powerful hard-line influence on foreign policy in Bush's first term. The political views of the two appeared to have been shaped when they worked together in the Ford administration in the mid-1970s. The lessons they appeared to take from that experience were at odds with the conventional wisdoms of the time. If the ignominious retreat from Vietnam had produced a widespread and long lasting aversion to the use of military force, at least except when that force was overwhelming as in Grenada or Panama, Cheney and Rumsfeld did not share that aversion. If a majority saw in the disgrace of Richard Nixon's aborted second term the need to restrain by law the power of the executive, they saw the presidency as being tied down by Lilliputian legislation and rulings that needed to be swept aside to fight the War on Terror.

The power that Cheney wielded in that office was probably unprecedented. His influence was evident in three main ways: through his unmatched access to the president's ear, through the extraordinary ubiquity of the bureaucracy he set up in his office whose members sat in on key decision-making meetings; and through his influence on appointments throughout the administration, most notably in the departments of defence and State.

The hawks that he was instrumental in bringing into the administration were of two types: those such as Rumsfeld, and John Bolton, undersecretary of State for arms control, who have been described as assertive nationalists, and those such as Paul Wolfowitz, deputy secretary of defence, and Douglas Feith, undersecretary of defence for policy, who are usually described as neo-conservatives. These two groups combined to introduce what came to be called the 'Bush doctrine', a policy prescription that used the 9/11 attacks to justify unilateral pre-emptive or even preventive military action by the US to deal with a threat before it had fully materialised. The 'doctrine' was encapsulated in a September 2002 national security strategy document, which provided a purported intellectual justification for the invasion of Iraq.

A third group in the administration, often called realists and epitomised by Colin Powell, Secretary of State, may have been unconvinced by the doctrine of preventive or pre-emptive war. But its members went along with the war in Iraq for a variety of reasons, some assuming that Saddam Hussein would sooner or later provoke the US into military action. While few realists were convinced that the justification existed for immediate action against Iraq, they did not oppose the invasion in principle.

The distinction among the hawks is important. Both groups shared a belief in US exceptionalism, the value of US military power, and a profound mistrust of international agreements and multilateral institutions and they joined to shape the way to war in Iraq, supported by liberals outside the administration who wanted to unseat the dictator. Critically, however, they split over the aftermath. The neo-conservatives saw the war as a first step towards spreading democracy throughout the Middle East, in part to help Israel, and to do that US forces needed to stay behind in Iraq to build democracy there. The assertive nationalists wanted to topple Saddam Hussein and leave quickly, possibly having inserted a US-friendly administration in his place. The coalition of hawks that had taken the nation to war thus had no identity of interest afterwards, helping to encourage the incoherence and vacillation that characterised the administration's actions once the regime had been ousted. Rumsfeld blocked efforts to send a larger force into the country to deal with any post-war chaos. Meanwhile, Pentagon planning for the post-war period was rudimentary, reflecting the department's lack of capacity for the task and the defence secretary's contempt for the State department, whose own extensive studies were ignored.

The indecision evident after the fall of Saddam Hussein was also a partial result of dysfunction within the administration. Bush said before taking office that he hoped for disagreement among the titans of his cabinet, because he knew such disagreement would be based upon solid thought. The president got his wish, but perhaps not with the beneficial outcomes he had anticipated. With Rumsfeld and Cheney on the one hand at loggerheads with Powell and his allies on the other, there was nobody to hold the ring. Condoleezza Rice, Bush's national security advisor, retreated from the policy formulation role that had been assumed by her immediate predecessors and restricted herself to a policy co-ordination function. But even with this more limited interpretation of her task, Rice struggled to rein in the cabinet's personalities and failed to prevent issues that had ostensibly been settled being returned to time and again. Meanwhile, although Bush characterised himself as 'the decider', a number of published accounts suggest his decisions were often taken without probing beneath the surface of the recommendations he received.

In retrospect, this combination of personalities and attitudes at the top of the Bush administration almost guaranteed that insufficient attention would be paid to the consequences of the invasion on a country brutalised by a quarter century of Saddam's dictatorship. Historians will differ on whether, given that recent past, an invasion of Iraq could ever have been mounted without provoking a bloody aftermath; what they will surely agree upon, however, is that for almost four years, US policy could hardly have been less effective in preventing it.

The least that can be said of the change in US policy that took place in 2007 was that it stopped reinforcing failure. A new counter-insurgency doctrine, based on highly evolved precedent that had previously been ignored and focused on improving the security of Iraqis, was adopted. The US temporarily built up troop numbers, by 50,000 to 180,000 at its peak, and began taking back neighbourhoods previously lost to insurgency and violence. This 'surge' coincided with a backlash among Sunni Arabs against the most extreme groups in their midst, allowing the US forces to combine with Sunni tribal leaders to push Al-Qa'ida terrorists out of areas in which they had previously thrived. A less noticed trend was the repudiation among the Shia of the most violent militia groups in their communities.

The resulting drop in violence took Iraq, at least temporarily, from the front pages of newspapers and meant the invasion became a less prominent issue in the 2008 presidential election campaign. The accompanying shift in popular perceptions reinforces the sense that impressions about longer-term consequences of the war for US policy have changed over time and are likely to change again. The war looked very different on 9 April 2003, when Saddam Hussein's statue was toppled before television cameras, in mid-2007, with the post-invasion violence in the country at its peak, and in early-2008, following the apparent success of the surge.

As with any policy action, including Iraq, the US political system will tend to reinforce what is seen to be successful, and (sometimes) react against that which is seen to fail. Yet Iraq does not stand on its own, but in the context of other actions by the Bush administration and the policies of successive administrations, many of which are informed by public attitudes.

So, while a widespread conclusion drawn from outside the United States might be that the notion of a pre-emptive war had been discredited by the Iraq invasion, it would not be safe to conclude that the idea has been comprehensively rejected inside the country. Indeed, from what can be judged from the comments of the three remaining presidential contenders in the 2008 campaign, John McCain, Hillary Clinton and Barack Obama, none has ruled out a future pre-emptive war. (Of course, it is questionable indeed whether the conflict could be properly defined as pre-emptive – given that nobody realistically claimed that Iraq's weapons of mass destruction, the invasion's stated *raison d'etre*, constituted an imminent threat to the United States or US allies in the Middle East. Thus, the invasion may be more properly described as 'preventive', a concept not easily justified in international law, and some will continue to insist it was purely aggressive in character.)

However, it does seem in 2008 that for the immediate future the bar for pre-emptive military action could well be set higher and that forthcoming US administrations will be much more sensitive to the charge that they are embarking on a 'war of choice'.

It is difficult to imagine, for example, any incoming government failing to heed advice from the professional military in the way that the Bush administration ignored military warnings about the inadequacy of troop numbers to handle post-invasion Iraq, and censured those, such as General Eric Shinseki, chief of the Army, who differed publicly from their conclusions. Indeed, the decision to implement the surge suggested the Bush administration was already listening more closely to influential army officers such as General David Petraeus, co-author of the Army's new counter-insurgency manual, once Rumsfeld departed from office in December 2006.

Similarly, the intelligence agencies, whose eagerness to please their 'clients' in the Bush administration and find evidence for Iraq's weapons of mass destruction provided formal justification for the war, can be expected to resist future efforts to manipulate their conclusions. Indeed, one important consequence of that already evident is the decision to publish the National Intelligence Estimate (NIE) on Iran in November 2007. The most startling conclusion of that document – the judgement that Iran had given up on nuclear weapons research efforts in 2003 even while it moved ahead on uranium enrichment – was distinctly unhelpful to US efforts to ratchet up international pressure on Iran over its nuclear programme, since it slowed down and diluted consensus on the need for further sanctions at the United Nations Security Council. Yet, it appears the decision to publish the NIE arose at least in part from the agencies' desire to regain credibility and the appearance of independence that was so seriously damaged in the run-up to the war.

Perhaps, however, the main constraint to future military action arising out of the Iraq war is its impact on the military itself, particularly the Army and Marines. Those consequences are the subject of a separate article, but the effects of tying down over 100,000 troops in Iraq for more than five years – as well as the intensifying difficulties in Afghanistan, where 25,000 US troops are now stationed – should not be underestimated. The extent to which the conflict has stretched those two services has been underlined by the fact that tours of duty to both countries have been extended to fifteen months – there are proposals to reduce this to twelve months later this year – and many experienced soldiers are on their third, fourth or fifth tours. Fully recovering from this tempo of activity will take the services many years, even in the face of the expansion of the Army (to a desired 547,000 by 2010) and the Marines (to 202,000).

One further conclusion widely drawn after the invasion, given the limited international support with which it was undertaken, was that the US should place more reliance on allies before embarking on military adventures. In the 2004 election campaign, John Kerry, the Democratic candidate, reflected this conclusion when he repeatedly emphasised the need to bring allies to the side of the US in Iraq. 'We need a fresh start, a new credibility, a president who can bring allies to our side', he said in a presidential debate on 30 September 2004.

At the time – with security inside Iraq in a dangerous downward spiral – it seemed an obvious retort to the unilateralist instincts of Bush and his cabinet, epitomised by Rumsfeld's adage: 'The mission determines the coalition. The coalition must not be permitted to determine the mission.'

But four years after Mr Kerry's remarks, as NATO struggles to build a coherent coalition in Afghanistan able to carry out its mission, the doubts about the wisdom of coalition warfare are resurfacing in Washington with a vengeance. From the vantage point of 2008, it is clear that the 'lessons' of the Iraq war, as seen in 2004, have been altered significantly by subsequent events.

It thus appears that the Bush administration's rush to war exaggerated trends that handled differently might not have appeared so marked, but some of those trends existed before and continue today. It should not be forgotten that Rumsfeld's comments were born in part out of the frustration with the restrictions placed by some European members that hampered NATO during 1990s' operations in the Balkans.

Indeed, the split between Europe and the US evident in the run-up to the Iraq war reflects in part a longstanding gulf over the utility of force. While oversimplified, Robert Kagan's argument that 'Americans are from Mars; Europeans are from Venus' characterises the differing approach to the question on either side of the Atlantic. Five years after the invasion, Europe is still regarded by many in the US as undertaking unilateral disarmament, and European governments unwilling to increase military spending or even modernise their armed forces. From the US perspective, this hesitancy shrinks Europe's influence – and therefore the West's – in world affairs in line with Frederick the Great's observation that 'diplomacy without force is like music without instruments'. Europe is thus viewed as enjoying the security benefits of American military power without paying the costs.

The unwillingness of European governments to spend money on the military in some cases reflects the difficulty of coalition politics, tight budgets and the growing demands on government spending from the social and other sectors. Yet, it is also true many governments (and probably electorates) in Europe are unpersuaded of the ability of military force to achieve its objectives, particularly given a complex networked world where the effects of military violence are instantly viewed in sitting rooms across the globe. From their perspective, the US too often acts like the man who, because he has a hammer, sees every problem as a nail.

Yet, Americans and Europeans are split over more than the importance of the military. One other gulf is over international law, viewed in Europe as of extraordinary importance but not always in the US, certainly not by most of the Bush administration. This suggests that even absent the Iraq war, important gaps would have opened between the US and Europe over the Bush administration's handling of the War on Terror, in spite of the initial agreement after 9/11 about the justification for military intervention in Afghanistan. If the cases of torture and prisoner abuse at Iraq's Abu Ghraib prison had not brought these differences to light, the treatment of individuals captured in the fight against terrorism – the questions raised by Guantanamo and secret Central Intelligence Agency prisons, the practice of waterboarding and extraordinary rendition of individuals to jurisdictions where they were likely to face torture – surely would have.

Yet although, as we have seen above, it was an unusual juxtaposition of personalities that took the US towards war in Iraq, their views arise out of longstanding American foreign policy traditions. They may have been opinionated exponents of those traditions but they are firmly within them.

The US foreign policy specialist, Walter Russell Mead, identifies the assertive nationalists (the term was coined by Ivo Daalder and James Lindsay of the Brookings Institution) as in the tradition of President Andrew Jackson. The Jacksonian view of foreign engagement, traceable Mead argues to that president's Scots-Irish 'back country' origins, favour a strong military but no longstanding international engagements. Bush himself, though not his father, appears firmly in this tradition. The neo-conservatives, meanwhile, represent a robust version of the tradition of President Woodrow Wilson, who saw American values as the answer to world peace and saw developing democracies as the way of spreading these values. (The two other traditions identified by Mead are those of Alexander Hamilton, the Treasury secretary, that favours international engagement to foster open markets and economic growth; and those of Thomas Jefferson, who are suspicious of international entanglements.)

One does not have to accept Mead's precise definitions to recognise that the hawks in the Bush administration articulated longstanding strands of thought in US foreign policy or to conclude that these views of the world will outlast the Bush administration. This clearly suggests that the tensions between Europe and the US generated by the war, as well as the wider loss of trust and respect around the world that it has provoked, will not disappear as a result of the mere arrival of another occupant of the White House.

Yet, given the contenders for the 2008 elections, some causes of confrontation seem likely to soften. While opinion polls show a substantial minority of Americans do not oppose torture of terrorist suspects, all three presidential contenders say they will ban the use of interrogation techniques such as waterboarding, which leads subjects to believe they are drowning. All three have also said they will close the internment facility at Guantanamo Bay. That will however leave a question, which may have to be discussed and resolved with allies, about how to handle terrorist suspects, since many Americans remain convinced that captured terrorist suspects are too dangerous to release, but believe those cases are not adequately covered by the Geneva convention or susceptible to resolution in civilian courts of law. Such steps are likely to form part of an effort to rebuild America's moral authority that has been seriously eroded during the Bush years.

The presidential challengers will of course face decisions on what to do in Iraq, and have promised different approaches, with John McCain and Hillary Clinton suggesting a longer-term commitment to the country and Barack Obama, the most likely Democratic nominee, promising he will pull US troops out in 2009. Whether this would survive his arrival in office is open to question, given that, as suggested earlier, future presidents may face increased pressure to listen more closely to military advice in matters military.

Obama has also said that, unlike Bush, he would talk to the leaders of Iran. In fact it is hard to see any US president sitting down with Mahmoud Ahmedinejad, the Iranian president. There is, of course, a question of whether any Iranian leader would see it as advantageous to enter a broad security discussion with Washington. As noted before, Iran has been a major strategic victor of the turmoil in Iraq, its position weakened only by the hopelessness of its internal economic management.

Just after the invasion of Iraq, Iran appears to have halted its nuclear programme. But it resumed uranium enrichment in 2006 and is now pushing ahead with that, contrary to the demands of the United Nations Security Council. It is moving ahead with development of its missile capabilities too as part of an effort to make it the dominant power in the Middle East. The ability of the US to deal militarily with a rising Iran – and thereby also to use the unspoken threat of military power to obtain diplomatic leverage over Tehran – has been severely constrained by the fact that so many military assets are tied up in neighbouring Iraq. Miscalculations by Iran – the capturing of US soldiers, for example, or an attack on a US naval vessel – could still bring about military action that could be justified before US public opinion and, to a lesser extent, the world's. But the space for a 'war of choice' against the Iranian regime, along the lines of that against Saddam Hussein, appears to have narrowed considerably.

This points to a final contradiction and perhaps the main consequence of the war in Iraq. If the war was meant by its protagonists to demonstrate that America could remake the world using the overwhelming power of its military, then the world may have drawn another lesson from it. The ease with which insurgents bogged down the world's most capable armed forces, combined with the weak co-ordination between the US civil and military authorities over the invasion's aftermath, badly dented the appearance of US invincibility. This is likely to have severely constrained the ability of the US armed forces to determine the outcome of future events or deter an adversary. The principal beneficiary of that development, five years after the invasion of Iraq, appears to be the theocracy of Iran.

There is little doubt that the manner in which the US went to war and the way the war was prosecuted damaged America's image, reducing its ability to lead by example and lessening its soft power around the globe. At the same time, the poor planning and setbacks suffered by the US military in Iraq battered America's hard power. That diminution of US power has left a vacuum that has allowed regional actors such as Iran and potential US competitors such as Russia and China to assert themselves more vigorously, with as yet unknown consequences. In short, because of the war in Iraq, America is less loved in the world and less feared than it was five years ago. The next president may be able to repair some of that damage, but is unlikely to reverse all of it. In retrospect then, historians may view 2003 as the high water mark of American power, the year the single superpower ceded its position and accelerated the creation of a multi-polar world.

4. Clarity Through a Dark Glass
Some American Lessons Learned in Iraq

Thomas Donnelly

Thomas Donnelly is Resident Fellow in Defence and National Security Studies at the American Enterprise Institute, Washington, DC. Among his recent books are *The Military We Need* (2005) and *Operation Iraqi Freedom: A Strategic Assessment* (2004).

Cataloguing the lessons – tactical, operational, strategic, political and even organisational – for the United States and more particularly the US military (and most particularly the US Army) is something that can only be judged over a generation. There is already something of an 'Iraq syndrome,' though exactly what it will turn out to be depends primarily on whether the war is won or lost. And from the vantage point of March 2008, that is an entirely open question. What looked to be hopelessly lost a year ago now looks like it might be won.

Indeed, many try to avoid the issue entirely: 'Tell me what victory looks like?' is still considered a clever question among the smart set. But the answer, to quote the theorist Foghorn Leghorn, is about as obvious as a hand grenade in a bowl of oatmeal. Victory is the creation of a stable and representative government in Baghdad and a long-term American ally in the project of reordering the greater Middle East. A tall task and a Long War, to be sure, but it is a definition that clarifies. It is also a way to grade what we have learned and perhaps not learned.

Back to the Future
The most obvious lessons that US military forces have had to learn, or more precisely relearn, are the ways of counter-insurgency warfare. It is difficult to judge how deep and lasting the commitment to these methods is; like most professional militaries, many in the US armed services still prefer to imagine war as they would like it to be rather than dealing with war as it is. The appeal of 'military transformation,' with its emphasis on long-range, precision strikes, remains intoxicating. And the legacy of 'capabilities-based' planning, a self-referentially myopic fad of the transformation years that measured not whether forces were useful against

enemies but whether they were better than they themselves had been – as though defence planning were a self-actualisation exercise – remains strong. As US Army Colonel H R McMaster, both a perceptive student of history and a successful combat commander in Iraq, has recently written:

> It is perhaps only natural that institutions and corporations that stand to benefit from a flawed concept of future conflict would find it difficult to divest themselves of a marketing a concept that has been successful and profitable in the past. Yet even the U.S. Army, despite having fought for six years under conditions that run counter to the body of ideas that drove [defence] transformation, is finding it difficult to cut loose from years of wrongheaded thinking. A recent Association of the United States Army pamphlet portrays the Army transformation efforts of the late 1990s as completely consistent with the experiences in Iraq and Afghanistan. The Army [vision of transformation], based mainly on computer simulations to validate a smaller, lighter, more efficient organization that could 'see first, act first, and finish decisively,' has not undergone any significant revision.[1]

And in at least the bureaucratic sense, the Army leadership has a point: they are obligated by formal strategy documents to prepare for contingencies along the full spectrum of conflict. It is thus difficult to make the system respond to the unanticipated demands of Iraq, Afghanistan or the broader 'Long War'. The bureaucratic inertia is magnified by twenty years of increased-but-unreflective 'jointness', which is to say increased centralisation of decision-making.

Yet it is remarkable how American soldiers and Marines have, mostly through bitter experience, managed to overcome these and other hurdles. The force that invaded Iraq with the idea of conducting the perfect blitzkrieg has, dare one say, transformed itself into one now enjoying remarkable success at a very complex counter-insurgency under twenty-first century conditions – not the least being instantaneous global media coverage and a battlefield that extends into cyberspace.

Rediscovering Counter-insurgency

Consider the case of Lieutenant General Raymond Odierno, who recently completed his tour as commander of all coalition forces in Iraq, and who, thanks to his role in making the Iraq 'surge' a success, has been promoted to full general and will become Army vice chief of staff. But, like so many Army and Marine officers, this was not Odierno's first tour in Iraq; his previous experience was as the commander of the 4th Infantry Division in 2003 and 2004. That division was the Army's most modern –

its most 'transformed' – with all kinds of new systems and capabilities. Thus, it was intended to be deployed through Turkey to attack into Iraq from the north, through Kurdistan toward Baghdad. When, as the date of the invasion neared, the Turks changed their minds about allowing this manoeuvre, the division sailed for the Persian Gulf and deployed through Kuwait at the tail end of the invasion. Sprinting to Baghdad with its antennas pinned back, the 4th Infantry arrived just after the fall of the Saddam statues, too late to participate in the immediate fight. Its first job was to relieve the units who had led the invasion on the front lines of occupation duty.

As that mission turned sour, the 4th Infantry and Odierno came in for mounting criticism: the division conducted massive sweeps, rounding up large numbers of detainees to no purpose (sending many of them to the Abu Ghraib facility), and was trigger-happy. Or so went the common view. These featured prominently in *Fiasco*, written by *Washington Post* military correspondent Thomas Ricks, and a book that did much to crystallise Washington opinion about what was wrong in Iraq. He quoted an internal division report concluding

> *Our unit has never trained for detention facility operations because our unit is neither designed nor intended for this mission... [My soldiers] are assigned a mission for which they are not trained, are not manned, are not equipped, are not supplied...and cannot effectively accomplish.*

The memorandum attributed these shortcomings to 'the command climate of the division as a whole', that is, at Odierno's feet.[2] The division's aggressive tactics were also a bone of contention with the Marine Corps. In a remarkable 2003 opinion piece in *The New York Times*, Lieutenant Colonel Carl E Mundy III, the son of a former commandant of the Marine Corps, sharply criticised the 'new get-tough strategy adopted by American forces in the Sunni triangle' and promised the Marines would reverse that strategy.[3] Whether this conventional wisdom was an accurate or nuanced representation of the situation in Iraq – and that argument still rages[4] – is less important than the fact that it was the accepted narrative in the US military.

The situation in Iraq was exponentially worse in late 2006 when Odierno assumed command of Multi-National Corps-Iraq. Since the bombing of the Shia mosque in Samarra the previous February, a sectarian civil war fought between Sunni militias backed and inspired by Al-Qa'ida and a variety of Shia militias including the Jaysh Al-Mahdi group led by firebrand cleric Muqtada Al-Sadr had brought the country to the brink of chaos. Three thousand civilians were dying each month and attacks on US and coalition forces topped 1,200 per week. In the United States, President George Bush's popularity had hit a nadir, the Republican Party had lost control of Congress in the November elections, Defense Secretary Donald Rumsfeld had resigned and the inside-the-Beltway elite had concluded the war was lost. All that seemed left was to negotiate the terms of an American withdrawal.

Odierno's job was to translate the counter-insurgency strategy developed by new Iraq commander General David Petraeus and employ the additional forces committed under the notorious troop 'surge'. Given Odierno's past public reputation, many in Washington believed he was the wrong commander at the wrong time. Yet

> When Gen. Odierno relinquished command of MNC-I on February 14, 2008, the civil war was over. Civilian casualties were down 60 percent, as were weekly attacks. [Al-Qa'ida in Iraq] had been driven from its safe havens in and around Baghdad and throughout Anbar and Diyala [provinces] and was attempting to reconstitute for a 'last stand' in Mosul – with Coalition and Iraqi forces in pursuit. The [Iraqi parliament] passed laws addressing de-Baathification, amnesty, provincial powers, and setting a date for provincial elections. The situation in Iraq had been utterly transformed.[5]

But as compelling as the story of Ray Odierno's personal Iraq redemption may be – the general himself is, perhaps not surprisingly, modest about the transformation of his public reputation and insists he is the same commander he has always been – he is a reflection of the kind of soul-searching that the challenges of Iraq and Afghanistan has produced among the American officer corps. The best-known expression of this intellectual struggle is the joint Army-Marine Corps counter-insurgency manual, produced under the leadership of Petraeus and Marine General James Mattis, one of the other handful of senior officers to distinguish himself in Iraq.[6] But the formal field manual is a trailing-edge indicator of the energetic and passionate discussions that have been taking place since the summer of 2003; it has long been apparent to junior officers and non-commissioned officers that US forces were imperfectly prepared for their mission; what has been less visible is what they have been doing about it. Presented on a day-to-day basis with the mounting evidence of the Iraqi insurgency, they recognised reality long before their superiors or the leaders of the Bush Administration would admit it. Much of the reporting, thinking, arguing and adaptation occurred out of the spotlight, on Internet sites like Companycommander.com and Platoonleader.org – originally soldier-built sites now incorporated by the military itself – soldier web logs and other such sites as smallwarsjournal.com or longwarjournal.org.

Whether the narrative of counter-insurgency transformation is a simple story of redemption is again less important than the fact that improvements on the ground are undeniable and substantial. Anecdotally, it is increasingly the case that those militaries who have worked most closely with American forces, notably British forces but also Canadian, acknowledge that the change is real; this is especially remarkable in the British case; it is rare to find much of the we've-been-doing-this-for-decades-in-Northern-Ireland *hauteur* these days. There is, of course, the question of whether the knowledge acquired at such cost will itself become regularised as revealed religion rather than evolving doctrine, or whether lessons learned in an ad hoc way result in changed force structures and procurements. For what it is worth, Odierno enters his job as Army vice chief with an appreciation that 'nation-building' is an 'unavoidable' mission for the service; he foresees counter-insurgency as the US Army's inevitable task for at 'least 20 years.' As he turns his attention to reorienting the service as an institution, his focus is on improving the quality and quantity of professional military education to prepare soldiers to succeed in complex battlefield environments.[7]

Redrawing the Art of Operations

The practice of the 'operational' level of war that had become a point of pride, possibly to the point of hubris, for American soldiers and Marines, and provided the intellectual framework for the post-Cold War renaissance of manoeuvre warfare in the US services, seemed to collapse like a house of cards following the capture of Baghdad. Some began to wonder if there ever had been an 'operational level' of warfare – tactics and strategy had been enough for Clausewitz – or whether the construct had merely served to justify the mushrooming of corps commanders and staffs or keep politicians from micromanaging military affairs. As one student at the Army's School of Advanced Military Studies concluded as early as 2003, '[T]he language of operational art was not designed for low-intensity conflict.'[8]

The rise of the defence transformation movement in the early years of the Bush Administration only served to exacerbate the disconnect between US land-force doctrine and the reality of counter-insurgency warfare. In particular, the concept of 'effects-based operations' (EBO), largely championed by air-power enthusiasts, did not translate well in the kinds of situations that American commanders faced from 2003 onward. Although allegedly an innovative doctrine, EBO seemed simply to be a hyper-effective model of attrition warfare; an argument that precise, simultaneous and sustained strikes could cripple enemy forces more rapidly than was previously possible. EBO begat a mania for 'rapid decisive operations'. In particular, the EBO school often severed the link between combat and politics. War became synonymous with battle; the idea of a strategic 'centre of gravity' – perhaps the single key concept in the traditional approach to the operational art – was supplanted by the thought that there were multiple centres of gravity. But again, these tended to be critical 'nodes' defined in strictly military terms rather than in terms of their political value. The shortcomings of this approach in a counter-insurgency environment were immediately apparent:

> *One of the largest deficiencies is the lack of examination of the creation of positive or enhancing effects. Nearly all the work done in EBO deals with the degradation of the enemy's system. However, in [counter-insurgency], the enhancement of your own system is usually critical, as is influencing and dominating uncommitted human terrain through the enhancing of the legitimacy of your system in the perception of the populace.*[9]

These deficiencies seemed to grow even more pronounced as the character of the current counter-insurgencies became apparent. The strategic ambitions of Al-Qa'ida and its associated movements have proven very difficult to come to terms with. Where they have attempted to govern, as in Taliban-era Afghanistan or in Iraq's Al-Anbar province, it has been relatively straightforward, if not easy, to separate the insurgents from the populace, as classical counter-insurgency theory recommends. The extreme nature of Al-Qa'ida inspired governance is its own worst enemy. Conversely, Al-Qa'ida can survive in 'ungoverned' spaces: Pakistan's Federally-Administered Tribal Areas, where the Al-Qa'ida senior leadership currently resides, provides the dictionary definition of an ungoverned space; there really isn't much of a 'host nation' to buttress. Moreover, the effects of globalisation, particularly in communications and even more so on the Internet, provide a 'virtual' kind of sanctuary and a more complex challenge by way of separating insurgents from the general populace.[10]

Generally speaking, where the US military and its allies can contest insurgents directly and prove themselves the more worthy protectors of the people, they have begun to enjoy significant successes. Indeed, these improvements are a measure of the revival of Odierno's reputation; it was Odierno who turned the Iraq surge into a practical victory. As Fred and Kim Kagan have recently and succinctly explained:

> [Odierno] believed that the surge allowed for 'simultaneous and sustained offensive operations, in partnership with the Iraqi Security Forces.' In conjunction with [Gen. David] Petraeus and his staff, Odierno planned and conducted three successive, large-scale military operations in 2007, and a fourth in early 2008. The first…dispersed U.S. and Iraqi troops throughout the capital in order to provide security for its inhabitants. The second…cleared al Qaeda in Iraq from its major sanctuaries. The third offensive …pursued AQI operatives and other enemies as they fled their sanctuaries and attempted to regroup in more remote areas. Odierno's last major offensive was…launched just weeks before his departure, to pursue the enemy into Diyala [Province] and set the conditions for the battle in Mosul – while providing essential services and jump-starting provincial government in less-contested areas.[11]

By counter-insurgency standards, Odierno's campaign was indeed remarkably rapid. By the same token, its successes in the clearing and initial holding phases can only be fulfilled over time. Because he has been promoted and transferred, the fate of his operational design is in the hands of others – and perhaps in the hands of the American electorate in the 2008 presidential campaign. And although the clearing operations involved some very heavy fighting, it was far from a pure application of precision firepower: the first military object of the campaign was to take ground, not to destroy enemy forces.

The questions of how to drive the enemy from the hills of Waziristan and from the pages of the Internet are more difficult. But while securing the Pakistani tribal areas would be risky and a tough challenge, clearing, holding and building in cyberspace, or in the minds of Muslims worldwide, is a qualitatively different task. One of the most significant shifts in US military thinking in the past five years has been recognition of the centrality of 'information operations' – an unfortunate term but one that reflects an increasingly nuanced understanding of modern war. The US Army, for example, in February 2008 published a new capstone manual on operations with this prominent passage:

> [Twenty-first century] conflicts occur in an operational environment of instant communications. Information systems are everywhere, exposure to news and opinion media is pervasive, the pace of change is increasing, and individual actions can have immediate strategic implications. At every level – from the U.S. Government and its strategic communication, through joint capabilities used to exploit and degrade enemy command and control, down to small-unit leaders meeting with village leaders – information shapes the operational environment. It is a critical, and sometimes the decisive, factor in campaigns and major operations. Effectively employed, information multiplies the effects of friendly successes. Mishandled or ignored, it can lead to devastating reversals.[12]

Iraq and US Strategy

In no arena will the distinction between victory and defeat in Iraq be so clearly visible than in that of US strategy. Iraq has been defined by the Bush Administration and is clearly seen in the region – and, in fact, globally – as a campaign in the so-called Long War, which itself is nothing less than an effort to shape a very different and more democratic political future across the Islamic world. And given the accelerating importance of the region to the globalised economy, and particular the great-power ambitions of India and China, the stakes could hardly be larger. This is not to be so hyperbolic as to say that as Iraq goes so goes the future of the planet, but it is fair to say that the outcome will do much to either sustain or dissolve the United States' position as the security lender of last resort.

The measures of defeat and its consequences are apparent; indeed, they formed much of the domestic political debate in the United States through the course of 2006, through that autumn's congressional elections, and into mid-2007. Iraq was said to be in civil war and becoming the front line in a larger, regional sectarian Shia-Sunni divide. More specifically, the Shia-led government in Iraq had replaced a regime that had once been Baathist-socialist but, in its last years, had begun to remodel itself as a defender of the Sunni. This change seemed to create a growing anxiety around the region and internationally. As Vali Nasr, then a professor at the US Naval Postgradutate School, wrote in his popular book *The Shia*

Revival:

> *The resurgence of the Shia-Sunni conflict feeds on the malaise at the heart of the Middle East's political and economic life, so much of which is marred by a persistent inability or unwillingness to negotiate over power peacefully and through regular channels. When change comes, it is abrupt and violent; what engineers call 'graceful,' as opposed to 'cataclysmic,' system transformation is a difficult thing to bring about in the Middle East.*[13]

Views of the irreconcilable nature of political troubles in Iraq and the Islamic world lay behind the prevailing wisdom in Washington. The consensus was well captured in the report of the Iraq Study Group, the bipartisan panel of former senior officials known as the Baker-Hamilton Commission after its two co-chairmen, James Baker, the former White House chief of staff in the administration of George H W Bush, and Lee Hamilton, former Democratic chairman of the House International Relations Committee. The report recommended a fundamental reorienting of US strategy in the region, a return to an offshore balancing of local powers, engagement with adversaries such as Iran and Syria, and a retreat from the 'freedom agenda' of George W Bush.[14]

From the perch of 2008, US prospects in Iraq look brighter. The Petraeus-Odierno campaign has greatly improved the security situation and a bottom-up form of political compromise has taken root in Iraq. In the Iraqi civil war, Al-Qa'ida Sunni extremists have been severely defeated if not yet destroyed (to the degree that these terms apply in a counter-insurgency environment) and the Shia militias have gone home – with the significant exceptions of those in and around the city of Basra and those 'secret cells' most directly connected to Iran. And the process of negotiating peacefully over power, through increasingly regular channels, appears to be genuine. To be sure, this process depends heavily on the continued engagement of the United States and the presence of US armed forces in Iraq. But Iraqis from all communities now want to build a long-term strategic partnership with the United States; they want, for the present, US forces to remain in Iraq (even if they want them to leave in some future day); and they recognise the American role as interlocutor in their internal process of renegotiating a durable domestic political compact. Iraqi nationalism, which seemed entirely dormant eighteen months ago, has reasserted itself and proved a hardier bloom than it once appeared to be.

If sustained, the recent successes of America's adventure in Iraq (and its adventure in Afghanistan) can still be said to hold the seeds of a profound power shift across the region. Beyond the immediate questions of the anti-terror campaign, and without indulging in the fantasy that representative governments in Baghdad or Kabul can have a magically transforming demonstration effect across the entire Islamic world, it would be a mistake to discount the willingness and ability of the United States to continue in its larger, Long War project. To be sure, the cost of the Iraq war has had a chastening effect; the United States is unlikely to again go to war as blithely as it did in 2003. But neither will it go to war so poorly prepared. Yes, American land forces have been stressed well beyond what was thought to be their design tolerances and the Army and Marine Corps remain too small to do all that they are asked to do. At the same time, as argued above, the lessons they have learned so painfully have forged them into a superb and remarkably flexible force: in addition to their newly-won competence in irregular warfare, the ability of US forces to deliver devastating fires and to project and sustain power over strategic distances endures.

Neither have the strategic interests of the United States in the Persian Gulf, the Arab Middle East or the larger world of Islam been diminished. And finally, Americans – Democrats and Republicans, conservatives and liberals – remain committed to a belief that the United States has a special role to play in the world. In the 4 March primaries, Senator John McCain clinched the Republican presidential nomination and Senator Barack Obama, despite his losses that night to Senator Hillary Clinton, moved closer to securing the number of delegates he needed to become the Democratic nominee. In their speeches that evening, both men, one after a final victory and the other after suffering a temporary setback, quoted Abraham Lincoln on America as the 'last, best hope of Earth'. As is so often the case, it is the continuities of American strategy that outlast the partisan differences or even the most grievous losses. Obama asked: 'Can we lead the community of nations in taking on the common threats of the 21st century? Yes we can.' McCain's rhetoric, typically, was more blunt, but the message was in many ways similar: 'We don't hide from history,' he said. 'We make history.'[15]

Notes

[1] H R McMaster, 'On War: Lessons to be Learned,' *Survival* (Vol. 50, No 1, February-March 2008), p. 24.

[2] Thomas E. Ricks, *Fiasco: The American Military Adventure in Iraq* (New York: Penguin Press, 2006), p. 283.

[3] Carl E Mundy, 'Spare the Rod, Save the Nation', *The New York Times*, 30 December 2003.

[4] Gian P Gentile, 'The Dogmas of War', *Armed Forces Journal*, December 2007, pp. 38-40.

[5] Frederick W Kagan and Kimberly Kagan, 'The Patton of Counterinsurgency', *The Weekly Standard*, 10 March 2008.

[6] *FM 3-24: Counterinsurgency*, US Army Training and Doctrine Command, (Fort Monroe, Virginia: September 2006), available at <https://akocomm.us.army.mil/usapa.asp?reason=denied_empty&script_name=/usapa/doctrine/DR_pubs/dr_c/pdf/fm3_25x26c1.pdf&path_info=/usapa/doctrine/DR_pubs/dr_c/pdf/fm3_25x26c1.pdfRef FM 3-24>.

[7] Author interview with Odierno, 3 March, 2008.

[8] Maj. Thomas Erik Miller, *Counterinsurgency and Operational Art: Is the Joint Campaign Planning Model Adequate?* School of Advanced Military Studies, United States Army Command and General Staff College, Fort Leavenworth, Kansas, 2002-2003, p. 69.

[9] Ibid, pp. 72-3.

[10] This point has been increasingly widely accepted, but this explication is derived largely from David Kilcullen, 'Counterinsurgency Redux', available at <http://smallwarsjournal.com/documents/kilcullen1.pdf>.

[11] Kagan and Kagan, op. cit.

[12] *FM 3-0: Operations* (Washington DC: Department of the Army, 2008), p. 7-1, available at <http://usacac.army.mil/cac2/repository/materials/FM3-0(FEB%202008).pdf>.

[13] Vali Nasr, *The Shia Revival: How Conflicts within Islam Will Shape the Future* (New York: W W Norton & Company, 2006), p. 28.

[14] See *The Report of the Iraq Study Group*, available at <http://www.usip.org/isg/iraq_study_group_report/report/1206/index.html; the so-called 'freedom agenda' was best expressed in President Bush's second inaugural speech, available at http://www.whitehouse.gov/inaugural/index.html>.

[15] The text of Obama's speech is available at <http://www.nytimes.com/2008/03/04/us/politics/04text-obama.html?pagewanted=2; the text of

McCain's speech is at http://www.nytimes.com/2008/03/04/us/politics/04text-mccain.html>.

5. Assessing the Surge
A RUSI Interview with Ambassador Ryan Crocker

His Excellency Ambassador Ryan Crocker is the US Ambassador to Iraq (March 2007 -).

'Iran needs to assess whether its current actions [in Iraq] are in its long-term interests. We're not prepared, given what they are doing, to offer them any more assurances, or indeed any assurances at all. In simple terms, Iran needs to 'knock this off' – and do so now, because their policy of deliberate violence against Iraq is something we consider very serious.'

On 18 September 2007 Ambassador Ryan Crocker visited RUSI after presenting his assessment of the 'surge' policy, with General David Petraeus, before the United States Congress. This is an edited account of the Ambassador's discussion with RUSI Director Professor Michael Clarke and *RUSI Journal* Editor Dr Terence McNamee

Michael Clarke (MC) – *What in your view are the connections between the military surge and the political filling of the vacuum in Iraq? What is filling in the footprint whilst the surge is ongoing?*

Ryan Crocker (RC) – The surge does not work purely by military means. The ultimate solutions in Iraq have to be political, and the surge is intended to create the space and the conditions for lasting political accommodation to be reached. We are seeing results of the surge that we did not, perhaps, anticipate before it began. What happened in Anbar province, for instance, would not have happened without the surge. The resolve and the success of the tribes to forcibly resist Al-Qa'ida in Anbar came about because they knew that the coalition was there in support of their efforts. Similarly in Abu Ghraib and districts of Baghdad and Diayala to the north-east, it is the same phenomenon. Because the surge is moving ahead and because it is working, we see elements of the Iraqi population (Sunni as well as some Shia) saying that they are done with extremists, done with militias – and they are calling for our support. The next step for us is to link that critical shift on the part of certain selected populations to the central government. We recognize that simply having the tribes in Anbar change sides does not fundamentally re-draw the political map for the better if there is no linkage to the central government.

MC – *That dynamic is in a sense not relevant in the South, where Al-Qa'ida isn't really the problem. It is not a question of buying the loyalty of the majority to throw out terrorists because there is a more indigenous disorder and insurgency in the southern areas of Iraq, where British forces are stationed. Would you agree?*

RC – Yes, but I think there are some parallels. Take for example the actions at the end of August in Kerbala, where extremist elements of Moqtada al-Sadr's Mahdi Army attacked the guards of the Kerbala shrine. In doing so they created a significant popular backlash against them. Thus we do see at least a resemblance to the shift in Anbar in the predominantly Shia provinces of the south. They too are increasingly intolerant of the extremist militias and turning to their own government and their own security forces for support. To the extent that this continues among both communities, it's clearly a positive development.

MC – *When you say they are turning to their own government, do you mean that they turn to the government in Baghdad or do they turn to their own local government? One of the problems of post-dictatorship societies around the world is that they have local politicians in huge numbers but none are truly national politicians who can unite the various communities.*

RC – That is one of the many challenges that Iraq faces. But there are strong indications that Prime Minister Maliki considers himself a national leader and indeed he has taken some fairly dramatic and courageous steps in Shia and Sunni areas, including his visits to Samara in the immediate aftermath of the June attack on the Golden Mosque and then in August to Kerbala right after the attacks on the shrine.

MC – *The government in Baghdad has to demonstrate competence not just to the people in Iraq but also to the American people. Therefore it must be a source of frustration for you that just when the surge reaches its peak (in numerical terms)* *the response from Baghdad is to ignore it. There is a sense that the there is a lack of urgency on the part of the Maliki government to meet some of the benchmarks they have signed up to.*

RC – Certainly there are 'two clocks', as we now say. The Washington clock and the Baghdad clock. The former is running much faster than the latter. Prime Minister Maliki has and is attempting to meet the benchmarks but these are complex pieces of legislation. And as I've tried to explain, as yet there isn't agreement among the major communities as to what the future shape of the state should be. Consequently, legislative issues become difficult to resolve in the context of the presupposed decentralized federal structure. Sunnis may be moving in that direction but when the draft legislation reached the cabinet they weren't at the table. It's critical that President Maliki keeps trying and persevering, and President Bush reminded him of that in their last conversation.

Terence McNamee (TM) – *What is your greatest challenge in dealing with the Iraqi political leadership? And what is your greatest fear on the governance and political leadership level?*

RC – The challenge I have in dealing with the Iraqi leadership is in a sense a reflection of the challenges they've got in trying to build a state. What happened in 2003 was not just regime change, it was the beginning of a thorough revolution. Basically everything post-2003 has to be developed from scratch. And it has to be done both against the enormous damage that Saddam did to Iraqi society and then the further damage that 2006 brought in terms of sectarian violence. So the Iraqi leadership's challenges in trying to shift state and society away from sectarian violence and toward some unified vision of what the future will look like are immense – as are the challenges facing the Coalition and myself, in figuring out how best to cajole, prod, push, encourage and improvise.

TM – *And if you widen that to the region, what would you ask of Iraq's neighbours in terms of them playing a more constructive role?*

RC – It varies. For Iraq's Arab neighbours, I would ask that they appreciate the fact that Iraq in its majority is an Arab society – and what happens in Iraq is important to Arab states as a whole, as they witnessed in so negative a way during Saddam Hussein's destructive reign. So it is imperative they engage constructively. There has been a tendency on the part of many of the Arab states to take a step back, unsure of the orientation of the Shia-led Iraqi government. I think that is a mistake. If Arab states are worried about Iranian influence, the best antidote is Arab engagement in support of this new Arab led Iraqi government, not distance. And that's why Saudi Arabia's decision to re open their Embassy in Baghdad is so important. For Iran, it is a different matter. Frankly, I think the Iranians need to take a deep breath and a long-term view both of their past with Iraq and (consequently) what best serves their future interests. I believe their stated policy is inaccurate, but their practice on the ground has not only caused problems for the Iraqis and the Coalition, it also serves to undercut their policy and puts at risk their long-term interests in Iraq.

MC – *With your background Ambassador, you understand the Iranian thinking better than anyone in the US foreign service. What therefore do you think the US could do in Iraq that would help engineer a change in Iranian perceptions? Paranoia in Tehran has only been reinforced by events in Iraq, whatever Washington says about its long-term aims in the region. Iran believes it is being surrounded and bases are being established to contain or attack Iran. What can the US do in Iraq that might change that perception?*

RC – Well, again, Iran has a long, rich history. It has perspectives and it needs to take advantage of those – again though, I would advise Tehran to take a deep breath and the long-term view. Post 9/11, Iran's two worst enemies have been eliminated: The Taliban in Afghanistan, against whom they almost went to war in 1999, and Saddam's regime in Iraq, with whom they fought an incredibly bloody, eight-year conflict. With these threats out of the way, Iran needs to assess whether its current actions are in its long-term interests. We're not prepared, given what they are doing, to offer them any more assurances, or indeed any assurances at all. In simple terms, Iran needs to 'knock this off' – and do so now, because their policy of deliberate violence against Iraq is something we consider very serious.

MC – *The trend of thinking among the public and the political elite in the UK is* *that we have to draw-down our military commitment in Iraq because of Afghanistan, and there is no longer the political commitment in Britain to re-making the Middle East as existed in the Blair government. If in reality Britain is disengaging from Iraq, what does the US want from Britain in the next eighteen months or two years? What is the best thing Britain can do from your perspective?*

RC – I was impressed by Prime Minister Gordon Brown's recent statement that Britain will live up to its commitments in Iraq and elsewhere because the stakes are high and they are important. With regard to the south-east, and Basra in particular, we are finally seeing signs that the Iraqi government is serious about the situation there and improving it, as evidenced by the appointment of two senior commanders: police and overall security commander. This is an indication that the Prime Minister understands the seriousness of the challenge to the state's authority in Basra. So I think it is important that Britain remain engaged, maintain significant force levels as a symbol of support and backing for this Iraqi effort, and that just as we are doing elsewhere in the country, changes in deployments need to be conditions based. The ability of Iraqi security forces to accept responsibility for the joint security station and Basra Palace are encouraging. Iraqis now need to move forward to show they can exercise authority throughout the Basra area and, as that happens, that's the context in which I believe decisions on forces levels should be taken.

MC – *From a longer term perspective, what sort of time-frame might you put on some stability in Iraq? Is this a generational thing? Or is there something we can look towards on a five- to ten-year time-frame? Regardless of the military engagement, what are we looking at?*

RC – This in my judgement is a very long-term proposition. The damage that Iraq has suffered over the past decades is going to take decades to fully overcome. That does not mean that turmoil and violence we are seeing now will persist for decades – not at all. Indeed I am hopeful that the success that the surge has generated can not only be protected but advanced on. The immediate challenge for Iraq and for Iraq's supporters is to bring the country to a position of sufficient stability and security so that the rest of the work can be done by political means rather than through street violence. That is the challenge because the process of political development is going to take many years. The challenge is simply changing the idiom of the debate from violence to political action.

MC – *And you are confident that Iraq will not split apart in that process or that it has a better chance of survival as a single entity rather than of fractionalization?*

RC – Yes, I do believe that. Polls suggest that the substantial majority of Iraqis want a unified state. I think that is true. Again, it is what kind of unified state that now needs to be determined and the nature of that debate needs again to move from the streets into political fora.

MC – *In the region, you often hear that the situation in Iraq was absolutely hopeless, but the nearer you are to Iraq, the more optimism you hear, perhaps because they believe that the 'project' of Iraq will continue come what may.*

RC – There is that optimism. Iraqis are tough folk and they have always had that reputation in the Middle East.

TM – *You have been very clear that there can be no let up in the intensity of the surge, otherwise failure is a very real possibility. But how deep is American political will for the surge and that level of commitment? Can it be sustained?*

RC – My sense is that if and when Americans become persuaded that the trajectory is on the right direction, then patience extends. Right now, the trajectory line is up, but it is only slight and it hasn't been so for very long. Iraqis need to demonstrate that they can continue this process. Again, I don't think anyone expects miracles at this stage, but to sustain engagement at or near the levels we are at now, people in the US need to see that Iraqis not only have the will but the ability to register progress.

6. The US Military after Iraq
A Speculation

Eliot Cohen

Eliot Cohen is Robert E. Osgood Professor of Strategic Studies, School of Advanced International Studies, Johns Hopkins University, Washington, DC., and is currently serving as Counselor to the U.S. State Department (March 2007 -). This article is drawn from Professor Cohen's contribution to a roundtable discussion at RUSI on 18 January 2006.

'In the wake of Vietnam, the view of senior officers was 'we don't do irregular warfare, it's not part of our repertoire'. And the same goes for peacekeeping. Neither was part of their understanding, or paradigm, of 'war'. I believe that has changed. Even soldiers from the traditional heavy army, such as the 1st Calvary Division at Fort Hood, with their acres of tanks and Bradley fighting vehicles, do not think of Iraq as anomalous. The sense now is that their tasks in Iraq will be the 'bread and butter' of future US military activity.'

What follows is not the product of intensive research or long periods of study. Rather, it is, as the title suggests, a *speculation* – based on my firsthand knowledge of the US military and many of its senior officers, and time (not a lot, but some) spent in Iraq – on a critical question: what will the US military, particularly the Army and the Marine Corps, be like after the insurgency in Iraq has run its course?

In examining this question, I do not address two issues which attract considerable interest in media and foreign capitals: the materiel or financial consequences of the war, and its specific implications for the US military – i.e., is the war going to break it? Neither, in my judgement, is especially relevant. Compared to all other countries' defence budgets, America's is staggering and, as such, is able to absorb myriad problems and shortfalls. And militaries, by and large, do not 'break' unless they suffer catastrophic defeat. That is not going to happen in Iraq. To be sure, there are signs of severe strain in the US military – divorce rates are up (though they have stabilized in the past year); recruitment and the quality of intake is down, if only slightly; and cases of Post-Traumatic Stress Disorder (PTSD) may be on the increase. Too many officers are being promoted at, say, the level of major or lieutenant colonel, too many soldiers with below average intelligence scores are being recruited.

Nevertheless, on a number of levels the indicators suggest a much more positive picture. One only has to recall Vietnam and the impressions given by soldiers – in the field and returned home – of that war. The stories of drug problems, depression, internal violence, an army fraying – you don't get that with veterans of the conflict in Iraq. The personal weblogs – fascinating windows on today's military world – reveal typical soldierly attitudes towards all manner of things, but not the sense of real decay and pointlessness that came to define soldiers' attitudes toward Vietnam. And lastly, for what it's worth, the reports I have received from my military friends in Iraq tend to be tepidly optimistic. No one is pretending that it will not be a long, hard slog. But the Iraqi military is improving, the US is doing a lot more counter-insurgency with them, and certain sectors of the country are becoming less violent – real signs of progress.

Iraq, Vietnam and Transformation

What particularly interests me is how the war will affect the temperament of the military. Will its understanding of the military profession be changed by the experience of Iraq? Large wars put an imprint on entire generations of officers. The US military was shaped by a generation from the Civil War, and so, too, the following century by officers who served in the Second World War. It was shaped yet again by Vietnam. I believe Iraq – with (to date) more than 2,000 Americans killed, 15,000 wounded and as many as a million soldiers having passed through the country – will define another generation of officers. Here the recent article in *Military Review* by Brigadier Nigel Aylwin-Foster, a senior British Army officer who was deputy commander of a programme to train the Iraqi military, is instructive. The article was, at least in part, a scathing indictment of not only the US Army but American military culture as a whole. There were suggestions of 'institutional racism', 'cultural insensitivity', 'a predisposition to offensive operations', 'a stiflingly hierarchical outlook'. Some of Aylwin-Foster's key charges were probably valid; others might be put down to Anglo-American tensions, or the particular period of his service in Iraq, or merely the differences between British and American military cultures. What seems abundantly clear is that in Iraq he encountered an American army shaped by the late Cold War, by its own reaction to Vietnam, and its overriding mission of preparing for large-scale combat in Europe. In this it was superbly proficient. But despite extensive formal military education, it had very little combat experience. By this time the Vietnam generation was washing out, and for the US Army the 1991 Gulf War – four days of combat against an enemy that was already largely on the run – was perhaps too brief to imprint itself on the current generation.

The same is not true of the insurgency in Iraq. Today's US Army is a battle hardened force. The 'combat patch', worn by soldiers to signify the unit they first went into combat with, is now virtually ubiquitous in the US Army. And they all know someone who has been shot at or blown up. They have experienced loss. Like their predecessors in Vietnam, they are unwilling to openly criticize their own institution and commanders, and the army that went into Iraq. As after Vietnam, there has been plenty of criticism directed at the offices of the Secretary of Defence, the State Department and so forth. But also as after Vietnam, there is an awareness of real failure by the institutions, and a resolution to deal with that failure.

Another comparison to be drawn with Vietnam is the Army's attitude towards 'irregular warfare', also known as counter-insurgency and a host of other terms. In the wake of Vietnam, the view of senior officers was 'we don't do irregular warfare it's not part of our repertoire'. And the same goes for peacekeeping. Neither was part of their understanding, or paradigm, of 'war'. I believe that has changed. Even soldiers from the traditional heavy army, such as the 1st Calvary Division at Fort Hood, with their acres of tanks and Bradley fighting vehicles, do not think of Iraq as anomalous. The sense now is that their tasks in Iraq will be the 'bread and butter' of future US military activity.

This leads me to the current buzzword in US and European military circles: transformation. I have never quite understood the concept (transforming from what to what?). What developments gave rise to the vague rhetoric of transformation is not especially important because it has, in my view, already been replaced by something very different, a much more focused approach to new military tasks. This approach to irregular warfare will be conditioned by experience and also technology. Whilst this will affect the Army and Marine Corps principally, other changes will bear more heavily on the Navy and Air Force, prominent among them will be the US-Chinese strategic relationship and halting the spread of WMD. The concept of pre-emption will, in turn, need to be considered much more seriously than it has been.

Civil-Military Relations

Equally significant as the changes in the US war-fighting paradigm are developments in the country's civil-military relations. American society has completed a process of reconciliation with its armed forces, mending the wounds that arose out of Vietnam. In the early 1990s, in the aftermath of the first Gulf War, the rapturous welcome given to returning soldiers partly reflected the deep sense of guilt Americans felt about the treatment of Vietnam veterans. As for soldiers, there were still lingering suspicions about being left in the lurch, that ordinary Americans did not understand or appreciate what they did. A number of developments have eroded these perceptions over time, but perhaps none more significantly than Iraq. The US military has taken serious casualties in an ambiguous cause for nearly three years, yet the support of American society for its military – however divisive the occupation has become at home – has been quite remarkable. This support is evident everywhere: at US airports, in restaurants, in the countless 'care packages' soldiers receive in the field, sent by people they have never met.

Support for the US military is resilient, but how representative is it of American society? Ethnically it is, contrary to foreign perceptions, fairly representative; socio-economically it is not. Officers who have attended elite universities are rare. After 2001 the current Administration could have changed that, but they failed to do so. That was a mistake, though a lot of the blame has to be placed on the doorstep of the military itself and its resistance to an aggressive change in its recruiting strategy. Increasingly, this military draws new recruits from military families, where sons and daughters follow their fathers and their father's father into the Services, as is common in Britain. There is no similar tradition in the United States, so it will be interesting to observe what long-term impact it might have on the military.

The relationship with the press is another area of civil-military affairs in which we are witnessing important changes. Within the military there remains – and always will remain – grumbling about individual journalists and the profession as a whole. On balance, however, the rancour and suspicion that blighted the relationship in the past is gone. The military has, broadly speaking, received fairly positive coverage; and it is a lot more sophisticated in its thinking about journalists – their role, their motivations, the differences between good ones and bad ones, who you can and cannot trust. Perhaps the greatest tension today lies not between the military and the press, but between the military and other institutions of government. Resentment is still high over the role of the State Department, the FBI and other agencies that failed to contribute significantly where and when they were needed once the major combat phase was over. The military is now far more attuned, and accepting, of the need for various kinds of involvement from government institutions and a much stronger inter agency approach to irregular warfare scenarios.

My last point on civil-military affairs centres on relations at the top, namely the relationship between the executive and senior commanders. In the 1990s a number of senior officers made no secret of their dislike for President Clinton. Indeed, some ought to have been court martialed, under Article 88 of the Uniform Code of Military Justice, for their publicly expressed contempt for the Commander-in-Chief. The fact that they were not – seen by many as evidence of his Administration's lack of backbone – only reinforced disdain for Clinton in the military. Much was expected of a Republican Administration, but when Defence Secretary Donald Rumsfeld demonstrated a brusque way with the uniformed military, and not much inclination to yield to their institutional preferences, a reaction set in. On the whole, this is a good thing: I would rather have a military that is slightly wary – not paranoid or fearful, but wary – of civilian politicians because it is all the more likely that they will be self-consciously apolitical. I would prefer not to see retired officers endorsing presidential candidates, as we have seen recently. More worrying still is the growing tendency of politicians to hide behind the military. It is not acceptable for any Secretary of Defence or President to duck criticism by saying that he/she is merely following the advice of military advisers or commanders in the field. That is a particularly insidious kind of obfuscation.

Conclusion

Iraq is going to leave an imprint – profound and lasting – on the current generation of young officers, who in time will be taking over the Army and the other Services. Iraq is also going to force the military to rethink its educational system; indeed, this is already happening. There is broad awareness that it did not do an adequate job of preparing the US military to fight this kind of war. The institutions of professional military education are not in good shape, and I am not convinced that they will get much better. On the other hand, there are a number of serious efforts underway to develop coherent military thought and doctrine to meet the challenge of irregular warfare, conducted by military people with firsthand experience. The Army is completely rewriting its counter-insurgency manual, and doing so along quite sensible lines. Moreover, there has been a real impetus to provide officers with solid post-graduate education. This was common during the early Cold War period, but in recent years the numbers of officers receiving post-graduate degrees has dropped sharply. Over the next year or two, with the introduction of new programmes, which among other incentives enables officers to take non-scientific degrees, including the social sciences and humanities, the numbers will jump dramatically. A remark by one of the most successful commanders in Iraq, David Petraeus, commander of 101st Airborne Division, reinforces my own view that this initiative will bear fruit. He told me recently that the most important training he received for dealing with what they encountered in the Mosel area of northern Iraq was not, as one might readily assume, his experience in Bosnia. Rather, it was having done a PhD at the Woodrow Wilson School at Princeton.

Besides the renewed emphasis on education, there is one final point that suggests that the US military is moving in the right direction and is beginning to grapple with the myriad complexities and challenges irregular warfare presents. And it brings us back to Brigadier Aylwin- Foster's article. No one in the US military could have read it without feeling uneasy.

However tactful, his message was blunt, and the verdict – on major aspects of US military culture – damning. Yet it was published in the flagship publication of the United States Army's Command and Staff College. It received the support of the head of the Army Training and

Doctrine Command, who had been a general officer in Iraq. Indeed, a copy of the article will reach every general officer in the US Army. It is this new kind of openness, and a capacity to accept criticism and learn from others that encourages me to believe that the United States is building a better and more thoughtful military for the future.

7. Reforming Iraq's Security Sector

Andrew Rathmell

Dr Rathmell is a director of Libra Advisory Group. From mid-2003 until mid-2004 he was Director of Policy Planning for the Coalition Provisional Authority (CPA) in Baghdad, where he was responsible for the CPA's strategic plan for the security and development of Iraq.

'The fact that the insurgents and terrorists are on the wrong side of history does not mean that they will inevitably be defeated. They clearly feel that they have the initiative and that it is the new Iraqi state that is under siege rather than the underground opposition. American and British statesmen and military commanders warned, rightly, that violence would escalate before the scheduled January 2005 elections. Unfortunately, they are probably not right when they argue that the elections will marginalize the opposition and enable a more legitimate government to restore order. The 'spoilers' are too powerful and the new Iraqi state is too weak.'

Tony Blair and George Bush have both declared that the war in Iraq pits democrats against murderous would-be dictators. Shorn of its evangelical rhetoric, this claim is true. The former Ba'athists, Islamist extremists and organized criminals orchestrating the violence in Iraq are fighting to prevent the emergence of a pluralist, democratic society governed according to the rule of law. The Shia clerics and assorted parties that make up the Interim Government are not liberals in the mould of John Stuart Mill or Thomas Jefferson but they are at least looking forward to a better future for most of their compatriots.

Unfortunately, the fact that the insurgents and terrorists are on the wrong side of history does not mean that they will inevitably be defeated. They clearly feel that they have the initiative and that it is the new Iraqi state that is under siege rather than the underground opposition. American and British statesmen and military commanders warned, rightly, that violence would escalate before the scheduled January 2005 elections. Unfortunately, they are probably not right when they argue that the elections will marginalize the opposition and enable a more legitimate government to restore order. The 'spoilers' are too powerful and the new Iraqi state is too weak.

Even before coalition troops entered Baghdad in April 2003, Washington and London were hoping that reconstituted Iraqi security forces would take over the policing of their country, allowing for a rapid withdrawal of international troops. This hope drives the accelerating efforts by the US and its allies to field Iraqi Security Forces (ISF), even as US and UK troop numbers are increased to make up for the all too evident weaknesses of the current ISF.

Some critics, including many Iraqi politicians, have lambasted the policy errors and programmatic delays that have dogged the effort to reconstruct the Iraqi security sector. American critics have pointed to the failed effort at 'Vietnamization' thirty years ago to argue that the international effort to build effective and sustainable security forces in support of a weak and corrupt government is doomed to failure.

We are where we are; few involved in Iraq would wish to start from here. We also have to acknowledge that the instruments available to the international community – the US military, the aid agencies and multilateral institutions – are not ideally suited to the task at hand. Nonetheless, flawed historical analogies are unhelpful – there is no disciplined, state-backed insurgency capable of seizing the Iraqi state by force. Instead, the task is to prevent Iraq collapsing into a failed, lawless state. This task requires sustained support for the Iraqi security sector and governance institutions but the international community also needs to be honest as to what it will be able to achieve. The task has only really begun and a multi-year commitment of blood and treasure will be required by the international community. At the same time, Iraq and its allies need to ensure that the security sector is fit to restore order but also does not unduly threaten transition to some form of democratic rule.

What Happened Under the Occupation?

Soon after the occupation of Iraq in April 2003, it became clear that pre-war assumptions about the likely security situation in Iraq had been wrong. The state, notably the police, was incapable of handling widespread criminality and banditry. At the same time, associates of the former regime and Sunni Islamists organized themselves into a formidable set of insurgent networks. The coalition had hoped to be able to assist the new Iraqi state to reform and reconstruct its security institutions to make them effective and accountable and so underpin a new, democratic Iraq. Instead, coalition forces and civilian administrators found themselves fighting a counter-insurgency campaign, rapidly deploying Iraqi security forces into the fray and simultaneously seeking to reform Iraq's broader security and justice sectors.

A great deal of heat has been generated by debates over the decision to dissolve the old Iraqi army in May 2003. With hindsight, it is arguable that a more gradual transition from the previous military to a new, democratic military would have been desirable. Certainly, a more structured process of disarmament, demobilization and reintegration, combined with political outreach to the Sunnis, would have been in order. However, far more significant was the decision to abolish the Ba'ath party and the myriad security and intelligence services. It was these institutions, not the army that maintained what passed for order in Saddamist Iraq. Dissolving them was necessary to ensure justice for the many victims of Saddam's crimes and to discourage the Shias from taking matters into their own hands. However, it should have been evident that no amount of foreign troops could fill the security and intelligence vacuum that the removal of these organs occasioned.

By the time the Coalition Provisional Authority (CPA) handed over authority to the Iraqi Interim Government on 28 June 2004, insurgent and terrorist violence was escalating, organized crime was flourishing and the security situation was threatening both the political transition and the reconstruction programme. The new Iraqi security forces and security sector institutions were embryonic at best.

Invalid Assumptions

Coalition pre-war planning had assumed a benign security environment and an Iraqi police force able to maintain order. When these assumptions proved invalid, the coalition struggled to maintain order and to improvise plans for the reconstruction and reform of the whole of Iraq's security sector. As with most instances of post-conflict reconstruction, the coalition was slow to mobilize the funds and personnel needed to support the fledgling Iraqi institutions. In any case, the coalition's plans had to be radically revised when the 15 November 2003 Agreement drastically shortened CPA's timeline.

In the face of expanding, multiple insurgencies, the coalition focused on rapidly fielding lightly-trained Iraqi forces. Whilst this increased the numbers of armed, uniformed Iraqis on the streets, it sometimes merely provided the insurgents with more soft targets. Thoroughgoing capacity building and institutional development proceeded in parallel but was less of a priority. By the end of the occupation, piecemeal progress had been made but it was only a start. This can be seen by reviewing the state of six elements of Iraq's security sector:

Iraqi national security institutions: CPA began too late but, by June 2004, it had helped Iraq's political leaders to establish national security institutions, most notably a Ministerial Committee on National Security. The Committee has been continued by Prime Minister Iyad Allawi but there is little sign yet of the development of true co-ordination between ministries at working level. Minister of State Qasim Daoud has begun to make good use of the Committee structures but their future will depend on the inclinations of the new prime minister after the elections.

The Defence Sector: The accelerated timeline forced on CPA by the 15 November Agreement left just half a year to build a Ministry of Defence (MoD) from scratch. A lot was done in terms of institutional design and recruitment of high calibre staff and the new MoD may serve Iraq well in the longer term if it is permitted to mature into a well-established organization. However, the institutional weaknesses of the MoD are a problem because the Iraqi Armed Forces are developing rapidly. This poses the risk that the armed forces will grow rapidly into a powerful institution, only nominally governed by a weak civilian ministry. This risk is exacerbated by the fact that, for understandable reasons, the new Iraqi Armed Forces are being used primarily as an internal security force, despite the best intentions of their founders and the stipulations of the interim constitution.

The Interior Ministry: The coalition sought to work with and reform the interior ministry and police rather than starting from scratch as with the military. This had the benefit of putting an Iraqi face on the security forces. The Iraqi police have, surprisingly, consistently topped the polls as one of the most respected of Iraqi institutions. Unfortunately, the Iraqi Police Service was never designed to deal with serious crime or political violence. As the lowest tier of Saddam's security forces, the police have struggled with their sudden transformation into the first line of the security effort. Now that massive amounts of US aid are flowing to the Iraqi police, the limited absorptive capacity and susceptibility to subversion and intimidation of a locally recruited force are becoming ever more evident.

The Justice Sector: Experience with security sector reconstruction and reform consistently demonstrates that building security forces is not enough by itself; strengthening the judicial and prison systems is vital if security is to be provided and a rule of law developed. The coalition worked to bolster and reform the criminal and civil justice systems but the sector never received the support it deserved.

A long-term programme of institutional development and training is still required. It is also vital that combined judicial law-enforcement institutions are developed that are able to confidently tackle organized and violent crime. The wider anti-corruption effort has only begun to take effect; there is no certainty it will succeed.

The Intelligence Services: The coalition was understandably reluctant to rebuild Iraqi intelligence services, preferring that future Iraqi governments deal with the morally and political tricky subject of how to build effective but accountable services. However, the worsening security situation meant that effective Iraqi services became vital. Unfortunately, the coalition began work on a reconstructed Iraqi intelligence community far too late, in poorly co-ordinated fashion.

DDR: Long experience with disarmament, demobilization and reintegration (DDR) in post-conflict situations was largely ignored by the CPA since it was felt that the armed forces had self-demobilized. A more structured and better-resourced approach towards former Iraqi military personnel would have been beneficial. In relation to militias, failure to give the transition and reintegration effort any discernible priority other than verbal support made success in this effort questionable from the start.

Developments since the Occupation

The (official) end of the occupation led to uncertainty over who was in charge in Iraq; although legal sovereignty was vested in the Iraqi Interim Government (IIG), it had little capacity to make or execute policy. This confusion gave the opposition the opportunity to go on the offensive and effectively take control of several cities over the summer of 2004. With better co-ordination, and the US elections out of the way, the IIG and the Multi National Forces were able to go on the offensive in the autumn.

The lack of effective Iraqi security forces, aside from a handful of special commando battalions, put the burden on the over-stretched coalition forces to undertake these offensives. Carried out in conjunction with political initiatives and reconstruction programmes, the offensives have had an impact. They have disrupted insurgent groups and removed safe havens such as Falluja. However, there are not enough coalition forces or reliable ISF to hold areas retaken, such as Samarra and Mosul, meaning that tactical successes cannot be translated into strategic victories. The challenge is exacerbated by insurgent successes at infiltrating and intimidating the ISF. Iraqi police and national guardsmen in Al-Anbar province in the West have been ineffective for some time but the more recent mass desertions of police in Mosul represent a major setback for the effort to build an effective and reliable police force.

Against this backdrop, an ambitious international programme to reconstruct and reform the Iraqi security sector remains in high gear – indeed it has accelerated since June 2004 with increased US funding and limited assistance from NATO and the EU. This programme largely builds on the efforts initiated during the occupation. The intention is to complete the core of the programme, deployment of trained, equipped and organized police and military forces, over the next eighteen months. This is however really just the start of a much longer-term effort to make the security sector effective and accountable.

Increasingly, the programme is being shaped by Iraqi leaders, but the security situation and the transient nature of the IIG and the Transitional National Government (TNG) mean that Iraqi leaders are unlikely to focus on long-term reforms anytime soon.

The Critical Role of Iraqi Leadership

The transitional administration scheduled to take office shortly will, like the IIG, be a caretaker government. Its task is to set the conditions for the constitutional convention, referendum and subsequent elections. It will inevitably fire-fight security crises as it goes along and concentrate on short-term, tangible indicators of progress in the security sector. However, it will be important that Iraqi leaders and their international advisors not become mesmerized by the fielding of large numbers of security forces. Whilst numbers are important, it is vital that they concentrate on building specific capabilities that will be necessary in the short term as well as investing in the security sector intangibles that will be of long-term significance. In the short term, they will need to continue to prioritize special commando units able to take the fight to the insurgents; they will also need to develop police-led intelligence units and joint judicial/police investigatory capabilities able to tackle serious organized criminals and terrorist groups. In the longer term, they will need to work on institutional development, notably the development of national security institutions and the ministries of defence and interior; creation of co-ordinated intelligence structures; and sustained support to the justice sector, including anti-corruption programmes.

As they deal with these apparently intractable challenges, the Iraqi leadership and their international advisors will also have to raise their gaze beyond implementing the current programmes and start to tackle some of the basic, unanswered questions surrounding the future of the sector.

These questions are essentially political. Throughout Iraq's history, the centre has used the security sector to coerce Iraq's regions and communities. In the face of the current security crisis, there will be a natural tendency to go down this route. If this tendency is to be avoided then there needs to be open debate and serious thought given to questions of centre-region relationships; state-society relationships; and the proportion of national resources allocated to security. Only by tackling these issues can Iraq's leaders ensure that the security sector both copes with the current crisis and provides a firm foundation for a well-governed, democratic state.

Unfortunately, we need to be realistic about the likelihood of the Transitional Government having the vision to tackle these strategic issues. Iraqi ministers and senior officials are likely to be more focused in coming months on their personal positions, even survival, than on long term institution building. The US, the UK and their international partners will have to work hard to ensure that long-term institution building remains on the Iraqi agenda, both with the government and with those who participate in the constitutional process in the coming year. This could mean a large-scale commitment of international forces, advisors and funds well into the second half of this decade. Building Iraq's security sector is the only honourable exit strategy that the US and UK have; it is not a strategy that will bring the troops home for Christmas.

The analysis in this article has benefited enormously from the work on Iraq of the author's colleagues, notably David Brannan, Jim Dobbins, Seth Jones, Terrence Kelly, Olga Oliker and Tom Sullivan but the conclusions are solely those of the author.

8. Security in Iraq

Jeremy Greenstock

Sir Jeremy Greenstock was the United Kingdom's Ambassador to the United Nations at the time of the US-led invasion of Iraq in March 2003. From September 2003 to March 2004 he served as the UK's Special Representative to Iraq. He is currently Director of the Ditchley Foundation. This article is based on remarks made at RUSI on 23 September 2004.

'We need to examine why the security situation is what it is now, why there is a very poor prospect that it will get better in the near future and what that is going to mean for the future of Iraq and the region.'

'If in your military philosophy you do not go to war unless you have overwhelming force on your side before you begin, and that is the case with the United States in any conceivable global situation, why on earth not over-insure in the situation after any conflict, when the problems may be more difficult in practice than during the conflict itself?'

Any discussion of this sort requires understanding backed with experience to sense the dynamic in Iraq and in the capitals we are dealing with. My analysis will focus on the security lessons that could be learnt. Such lessons will not necessarily have been or will in the future be drawn on by those who have been through the Iraq experience. However, they point to one or two things that are quite important in terms of learning from what we have been doing over the last eighteen months.

Recent Background

Let us begin with some assessment of what has brought about the present situation. I was one of those who accepted the basis for taking on Saddam Hussein militarily. After the adoption of United Nations Security Council Resolution 1441 there was legality in what we did; the resolutions are there. Whilst people may have tried to re-interpret those resolutions, I am clear in my own mind about this. I would otherwise not have continued to support the US/UK action. But whether it was legitimate or not to a large extent in the end has to be justified by the results of what we did.

The advantages of our action include a confidence that Iraq cannot threaten us again with Weapons of Mass Destruction (WMD). One may scoff at this idea, but we did not know at the time that Iraq was not a threat with WMD, and everything pointed to the fact that they were concealing things which could have been dangerous. Saddam was in no doubt himself that he was defying the UN. He was relying on something else to avoid a military invasion by the US. The UN knew, we knew and he knew that he had not fulfilled his obligations under the resolutions. The second advantage is that Saddam himself has gone: it was not the reason why the UK used military force in Iraq, but the fact that Saddam has gone is still high in the minds of most Iraqis as a plus. If there are minuses in their minds, it is not that they want Saddam back. Or that they regret the creation of an opportunity for a different, free, independent, federal, democratic Iraq as in the Transitional Law of 8 March 2004.

Thirdly, we are learning in some respects that Iraq is not a bad place for political reform in the Middle East. Whilst the issue of democratic reform in the Middle East is a province for another discussion, it is worth pointing out that reform has to come from the wishes, aspirations and the decisions of the Arab peoples themselves. It cannot come from outside, and it will come in the style of the people in each national territory. It does not have to be a democracy in the Western sense: I prefer to make the objective government with the direct consent of the people.

Another advantage coming out of the period of the Coalition Provisional Authority (CPA) was the political transition process itself. It was a very sensible eighteen-month transition process which I think the Iraqi people were perfectly happy with, remain happy with and want to see fulfilled.

The deficiencies are almost all wrapped up in the security situation. Posit a benign security situation and everything else we have planned would be working perfectly well. That is the huge proviso, given what has happened. But we need to examine why the security situation is what it is now, why there is a very poor prospect that it will get better in the near future and what that is going to mean for the future of Iraq and the region.

Mistakes

Let me be reasonably straightforward about some of the mistakes that were made that fed into a poor security situation now. It is built around my contention – maybe with a touch of hindsight here, but it is nevertheless a powerful point – that if in your military philosophy you do not go to war unless you have overwhelming force on your side before you begin, and that is the case with the United States in any conceivable global situation, why on earth not over insure in the situation after any conflict, when the problems may be more difficult in practice than during the conflict itself? If you over-insure for conflict why do you not over-insure for the immediate post-conflict situation where you are most likely to lose control of the security situation.

In Iraq there were two things in particular that happened. First, there was a mis-analysis of what Iraq would be like after the removal of Saddam. The analysis of that was not fully discussed within the administrations involved, particularly not in the American administration, when there were papers, there were people, there was potential for debate. The result could have brought out, at least as a scenario option for discussion, how difficult Iraq might be after the despotic repression that Saddam represented.

After that mis-analysis, and perhaps as a result of it, there was then an under-resourcing of the security control immediately after the conflict was over. I think everybody was shocked – I was shocked at a distance – at the looting and sabotage that came out of the Iraqi population – an expression of anger against Saddam, not against the Americans or the British. But it was ruinous in two senses. It destroyed infrastructure, ministries, cultural places and a lot of other things. It also signalled that there was to some extent a security vacuum. There were no police on the streets to stop that sort of thing and it led to a period where the Saddam remnants and the beginnings of foreign terrorism in Iraq were attempting to establish an effective presence on the ground. There were too few security operators on the ground in terms of a classic security structure for a state like Iraq, for law and order to be established in those early months. Lessons were subsequently learned by the opposition which they have built on since, becoming more sophisticated, faster than has the defence. This has stemmed from an under-resourcing from the beginning.

There are two examples. In the first instance: the borders were wide open and so new terrorists could come in and join the Al-Qa'ida franchise or join the Ba'athist opposition if they wanted to without any particular problems. Secondly: the ammunition dumps that Saddam had created for his own forces had as much ordnance on the ground as the whole of the US army on the soil of the USA – one and a half million tonnes of it. It was available for filtering out into the population at large. No attempt was made in the early stages to close the borders or deal with those dumps because there was only a finite number of effective troops on the ground, under orders from headquarters, and those things were regarded as of less priority.

Whilst current administrations may not necessarily learn from the experience of the British in Iraq in the 1920s and 1930s, the inference can be drawn that if you start light and have to increase the pressure on a territory to keep security, you will lose hearts and minds. If you start heavy and progressively, as you ensure control, you lessen the outward signs of control, then you will carry the population with you. I think we got it wrong in terms of that progression.

British Experience

As for the British experience, in Basra and the four southern provinces we handled things in certain different ways in the early stages and onwards. I think there are lessons that could be drawn from that which would be valuable for other countries as well. That said, one should remember that the Shia south was a more cohesive, more settled area in political and security terms than the rest of the country, Kurdistan apart. It was more opposed to the centre, both to Saddam and indeed out of a natural southern specialness to the post-Saddam centre. The British were able to capitalize on a community that quickly got its act together to decide that they wanted to work with the foreign security forces in their midst, and get society going again. And a certain virtuous cycle was generated by the British, whereby they reached out to the population, they went out to the municipal leaders early on, they took off their outer armour and patrolled in a more friendly way. Brave stuff for those who did it, but it saved lives later. The population on the whole realized that these people were working with them and began to inform on people from outside the region who were coming in to break up law and order. Hence a cycle composed of contact, hope for the future, understanding of the relative interests of the local population and foreigners alike, a wish to keep that going, and effective means to inform on and combat the opposition. So that the thing got better.

Terrorism, and to some extent Ba'athism and to a smaller extent things creeping across the border from Iran, tried to disrupt that process in the south and at times got through. There have been a small number of really nasty incidents in Basra. But on the whole the process worked quite well. The Americans may not necessarily have got it all wrong in the other areas, where conditions were much more difficult. They dealt with much more disparate communities and with a very disaffected, angry, frightened Sunni community in the Sunni heartland. There was immense courage, very good planning from swathes of the American military, and individual commanding of distinction including in the north-west under Petraeus and in the centre-north under Swannack. Brilliant stuff. But in terms of blocking the opposition's linkages between the different areas, dealing with the people of violence and denying them safe areas from which to act against the central administration, it was not enough; that virtuous cycle was never generated. That has meant a fairly steady leakage of political and popular support for what we were trying to do, because law and order amongst the population was the most important thing they were looking for. When that was compounded by the stories of prisoner abuse, it became very difficult to hold that leakage. The average Iraqi perception is that they felt increasingly humiliated by the presence of foreign troops. Humiliated by Saddam, humiliated by the method of Saddam's removal because they did not do it themselves (the Americans of all people did it), humiliated by the fact that they could not restore their lives quickly after the event. Those underlying currents of resentment, anger and frustration obviously were going to come out in some parts of the population as a wish to use weaponry and to kill people.

Dealing with the Terrorists and Insurgents

The situation we now face is extremely difficult. There was a comment in the press that the coalition forces are only in control of the ground they occupy at any given time. To some extent that is true. But it is also true for the insurgents and the terrorists. (By insurgents I mean Iraqis who want to stop this transition process, by terrorists I mean the non-Iraqi Al-

Qa'ida franchise.) They too only control the territory they are physically on at any moment. Neither knows necessarily where the other is going to be in the next day's planning. If that is the case, in security terms, each of those two sides only dominates the area where they are actually present at any one moment. Of course, if they happen to be in the same area and they meet, the larger will beat the smaller.

What is happening in the rest of Iraq, where neither of them are? The answer is a good deal of normal living is going on. The oil sector has not been that much disrupted by the sabotage. Electricity supply has been disappointing but it is now increasing again. Markets are crowded and traffic is jamming the streets. In parts of Iraq, local democracy has already started to take root, in elections for governors and municipal leaders. That is certainly the experience of the British in much of the south-east.

What has to be done now is clear. With the Iraqis in the lead, this area of uncertainty in the middle has to be brought over, in both security and political terms, to the right side.

The analysis has not been careful enough in this respect partly because the coalition forces are always, in my experience anyway, over-stating their expectations, over-stating the control that they actually have. There is no careful analysis of the downsides of what is happening and how they should be dealing with them. But if there is neutral ground to be won, the Iraqi government and the foreign forces supporting them should be out there doing it. They should set up a political process that the people will be interested in. They should be trying to stop movement between areas where they know that insurgency activity will be trying to connect. They should seek to get aid and reconstruction projects into sensitive areas very quickly. Here there has been a failure to disburse the sums of money that were supposed to be available from donors, not least the US $18 billion. Of that $18 billion, so far $600 million has been spent in 2004. It is not enough. Now that the State Department are in charge, that is being accelerated. In my *Economist* article in May, I stated that there were two performance indicators that are interlinked: security and jobs. Security partly comes from a population that is beginning to be re-employed, that places a value in its own future and that begins to work for that future, acting against criminality and insecurity in their communities. But if they have no hope for the future, if they are not being looked after by the state, they will not give the state back their loyalty, in terms of making sure that security has to be dealt with within their community and that people who are using violence are excised from their community.

There should be a focus on what is going to stop insurgents and terrorists building their constituency further. They have advanced too far over recent months. I am not going into further detail, because counter-insurgency policy needs a very particular approach. Perhaps Prime Minister Allawi is forming this in his Supreme Policy Council. But there has not been enough clarity in the public pronouncements of those who are responsible for the situation on the ground to show that this is what they are doing and to give confidence that they have got a policy that is going to work.

Now, with the awful events in our headlines in the last weeks of September, showing how individuals can be subject to the brutality that Al-Qa'ida is capable of, but also thinking about the wider implications of the spread of terrorism and about the motivation for terrorism coming into our own societies, we can learn lessons from what terrorism has done on the soil of Iraq so far. In my view, events in Iraq have not been a cause of greater international terrorism, rather a symptom of it. Such terrorism was already motivated by events previously. By the Bin Laden successes; by the failure to capture Osama after the Afghanistan campaign; and by other incidents that have happened around the world. Iraq was just another place where terrorism was able to migrate to in order to secure what it saw as successes. But Iraq has become an extremely important symptom of international terrorism: to the point where it is absolutely essential that we win the battle against terrorism in Iraq. Otherwise that motivation will be redoubled and there will be a territory from which terrorism can act. It would be able to operate in a particularly dangerous and geo-politically important region, using people who are learning new methods all the time.

But there is another side to this. The response to terrorism cannot be 100 per cent a military response. Power in the world is no longer just military or economic power. As the world gets freer, in all sorts of respects, policy implementation also needs persuasion; legitimacy gained through credibility and persuasion. If you have not convinced a population that the violence on their soil has to be eradicated in their own interests, you are not going to get rid of that phenomenon in that territory. The whole point of the Counter-Terrorism Committee of the Security Council, following Resolution 1373 in September 2001, was to make every member of the UN realize that they had to raise their own capability to keep terrorism off their soil, so that terrorism had nowhere to go.

If that was applied rigorously and well through US leadership at the UN in 2001, why was it not applied within Iraq? For the people to reject terrorism, for terrorism to disappear from a society, requires a lot more than military power or money. You are into amorphous things like a belief in the future of your country, the right sort of nationalism, a belief in values from which violence is excluded. There are global implications in what we are learning as things evolve in Iraq. They have to be worked through. Commenting briefly on the recent spate of hostage taking, one can see that this is becoming an extra weapon of terrorism that we are going to have to deal with. It will not necessarily be a phenomenon only in highly insecure areas.

Iraq's Neighbours

A final word about Iraq's neighbours. Iraq operates in an important region and Baghdad is undergoing a significant series of conversations with its neighbours on regional stability and on reconstituting a normal regional life between them. But clearly, although none of the neighbours are going to be primary deciders of the way things go in Iraq, particularly Iran in that context, they all have very important roles. Turkey is obviously interested in what happens in Northern Iraq and Kurdistan; and all the neighbours would have something to say and reactions to carry out according to what happens on the ground in Iraq. As for the Iranians, I do not think that they want the situation in Iraq to be so unstable that they witness their neighbour going through the same process of chaos, leading to another dictator who might be a highly insecure neighbour to their west. But neither do they want things to go so well in Iraq that the US in particular feels 'we can do this, this is something that has worked, and therefore we can apply the same model to anybody else who we decide is not following the policies of global security as we see them'. From Tehran's viewpoint there will be those who say let's not make it too easy, let us do certain things that just keep the difficulties ticking over. Furthermore Iran is reacting to the Iraq experience in its own responses to other matters, say the development of nuclear materials, and they may make decisions which are affected by their judgement of the US presence in Iraq.

Transition and the Future

So events in Iraq have wider connotations. They are connected with global issues like the role of the single superpower; the role of the UN; ways of dealing with WMD and with terrorism; with the regional dynamic; and with the way Palestine has to be dealt with in the future – Iraq is cross-connected with all sorts of things. But unless you get the internal situation in Iraq right, you will not be able to deal with those other issues in the way in which it would be best in your interests to do so.

There is of course a danger of other things happening in the region, not excluding Iran, which could feed back into the Iraq situation. It could be a two-way dynamic. But it is a situation at the moment which has enough difficulties in it for us to be extremely concerned about its course. As a result of that, it is important that the elections in Iraq should be held on time, or at least within the first half of next year, for one overwhelming reason: violence should not be allowed to dictate how the state is going to deal with violence. Violence can only be eradicated through a people and a government working together to eradicate it. It cannot be done by the government alone. It cannot be done by people with no confidence in government. A government that moves, as was intended, beyond the interim period to an elected assembly which gives authority to a new government in the second part of the transitional period is to my mind an essential tool for continuing to deal with the violence on Iraqi soil. Therefore I do not agree with those who say that perhaps the security situation is too bad for elections. It will be too bad in certain areas; and maybe that will have to be accepted as the high cost of Iraq going through this transition period. But not to have elections is a concession to violence and an admission that violence has won a victory. That to my mind cannot be allowed to happen.

Terrorism and the insurgency are not really offering political alternatives to Iraq that interest the Iraqi people. However, the cost of going through this stage, given the progression of events, has got to be borne by the Iraqi people. In addition, it contributes to overall progress in giving the Arab peoples a voice in their own future to make sure that violence does not win across a much wider swathe of global territory. That is why the Iraqi people need support in their present crisis, whatever your feelings about the origins of the conflict. That is why we have to keep going through the whole transitional period in Iraq.

August 2003, RUSI Journal, Vol. 148, No. 4

9. Military and the Media

Richard Sambrook

Richard Sambrook is Director of the BBC's Global News division. This article is based on his address to RUSI on 20 June 2003.

'We reflected what we heard and what we were told, and the way the military, the government and the country were feeling about the war. Before the [Iraq] conflict we reported many of the briefings which anticipated a rapid and easy victory ('a cakewalk'). Expectations were deliberately raised.'

In many ways Iraq must have been one of the easiest wars to win – an unrivalled military superpower with high tech weaponry pitched against the remnants of a dictatorship with outdated equipment. For the media it was – statistically – the most dangerous of wars to cover: fifteen dead and two still missing in just four weeks.

The speed with which the war was won gave us no time to reflect on the complexity of the new kind of relationship that was forged there between the military and the media. But as we start to think about these issues, I realize we've barely begun to recognize the problems of reporting modern warfare. Crucially, I don't believe governments or the military have yet recognized the consequences of war in a wired, globalized, media-rich world.

There is an inevitable tension between the military and the media. The military want to win; the media want to find out the truth. It is of course possible for both to do their jobs in the best and most honourable ways and still be in conflict. That's part of living in a democracy.

In twenty-five years as a broadcast journalist I have seen the techniques of both fighting and reporting change, from the Falklands, to the Gulf, Kosovo, Afghanistan and Iraq. Now running the world's biggest broadcast news organisation, I believe the tensions between the military and the media are getting a lot more complicated. The war in Iraq has made the uneasy relationship between military and media more difficult than ever.

For the media, the war is good business. TV and radio audiences go up, newspapers sell more copies. News is best at reporting events and war is an event on a grand scale, with winners and losers, heroes and villains. For the military news coverage – if all goes well – ensures public support and undermines enemy morale. And since the 1991 Gulf War, global twenty-four hour media has meant information planning has become an increasingly important part of military planning. NATO spokesman Jamie Shea said after Kosovo, 'without pictures there can be no news and you can talk endlessly about battles won but people will not believe them until they have seen the pictures.' And so TV in particular has become part of the psychological battle. And that pushes us unwillingly from being observers to participants. As Douglas Hurd said in 1993, 'the public debate is run not by events but by the coverage of events.' This is where our problems start.

I think Lord Hurd's view goes a long way to explain the thinking behind the 'embedded' reporters in Iraq. Capture the day's pictures and you capture the narrative of the war. If only it were that simple.

Embedded Journalists

I have never been in a war. But I know enough to understand that news coverage can never reflect the real thing. A news report is inevitably imperfect – condensed, packaged, and affected by a wide range of influences. In Iraq the embedded system raised many questions about journalistic integrity or independence. My initial impression is that in practice those issues weren't a major problem for the media. By and large we were able to broadcast whatever we wanted. The real difference came in the sheer numbers of journalists accredited and in the technology which allowed them to 'go live'.

The BBC has commissioned some independent academic research from Cardiff University into the role of embedded reporters, what they brought to the coverage and what they didn't. We'll see what they conclude. That said, for many millions of people, the front line access in Iraq provided a more authentic sense of battle than they have ever been exposed to before, including the 'fog of war'.

Embedded journalists certainly captured something of the experience of the average soldier – the professionalism of course, but also, at times, the disorientation and confusion (i.e., the human face of war). And that seems to me to be a very healthy development. But it wasn't always reassuring for audiences at home looking for certainty.

Editing a TV news programme twenty years ago meant you had time to check facts, reach judgements and put together an account of the day which you understood to be fair and accurate. Today, the editors on 24-hour news channels do not have that luxury. The audience is alongside them as they receive first reports, which are often wrong, and try to make sense of what is – and is not – going on. The viewers are further up the information chain, getting information sooner and at their convenience, but also witnessing live the process of assessment and judgement.

That is a fundamental change to the experience of watching TV News. This was compounded by live coverage from embedded reporters.

In the Falklands there were just twenty-nine British journalists dispatched with the navy. Their reports were subject to military censorship and often not transmitted for several days after an event. In Iraq there were 2500 journalists, many able to broadcast live the rumour and confusion of the front line. Satellite phones, mini cameras, laptops and more facilitate speed of reporting to a public anxious for news. Reporting from the front line has also moved up the information chain, often ahead of what is known in military headquarters.

Put these two together and what you *don't* get is guaranteed accuracy or authority, live in the nation's living rooms. You get a vivid snapshot of one moment at one place in the battle – war through the keyhole. Or as one American journalist put it,

You were somewhat like the second dog on the dogsled team and you saw an awful lot of the dog in front and little bit to the left and right. But if you saw an interesting story to the left or right you couldn't break out of the dogsled team without losing your place…

Embedded reporters were intended to capture the narrative and the adrenaline of the front line. But they could only ever be one element in the media's attempt to find out what was really happening. Therefore, as a journalist trying to report the war, you know you have to supplement the front line reporting. Which is where the tensions in this uneasy marriage get twisted further. In trying to put together the jigsaw picture of the war there are at least three other elements.

Unilateral Reporter

The 'unilateral' reporter is one who is not accredited but works independently. In the 1991 Gulf War journalists working this way produced some of the most important reports. But since then, in Kosovo, Afghanistan and Iraq it has been phenomenally dangerous to work this way. The death of Terry Lloyd of ITN and the deaths of two BBC team members in northern Iraq were salutary reminders and inhibited more unilateral reporting. And here we step onto difficult ground.

Working independently is the journalist's ideal. But it is not in the interests of the military. We can get in the way, journalistic casualties take up time, energy and focus, and we will probably be 'off message'. The uncomfortable facts are that in Iraq most of the media staff killed were working unilaterally, and most of them were killed by 'friendly fire'. This has led to a degree of suspicion or perhaps paranoia in some parts of the media. Some believe the Pentagon's attitude to war correspondents is the same as President Bush's when declaring war on terrorists: 'You're either with us or against us'. As the writer Philip Knightley said recently in *The Observer*:

> Journalists prepared to get on side – and that means 100 per cent on side – will become Embeds and get every assistance. Any who follow an objective independent path, the so called unilaterals, will be shunned and those who report from the enemy side will risk being shot.

Martin Bell, a man with much experience of war reporting, remarked:

> I think it's very worrying that independent witnessing of war is becoming increasingly dangerous and this may be the end of it. I have a feeling that independent journalists have become a target because the management of the information war has become a higher priority than ever.

If men like Knightley and Bell are worried, then I think there is cause for concern.

Within media circles, this view has been compounded by attacks on Al Jazeera's offices in Kabul and Baghdad, the shelling of the Palestine Hotel in Baghdad, and by the antagonism of Washington and Downing St. to anyone trying to report from Baghdad. Rear Admiral Craig Quigley was frank about this after Afghanistan. He said the Pentagon was indifferent to media activity in territory controlled by the enemy.

The Al Jazeera bureau in Kabul was shelled because the Pentagon said it had 'repeatedly been the location of significant Al-Qa'ida activity'. It seems this may have been the regular interviewing of Taliban officials, something Al Jazeera thought was normal journalism.

The Pentagon and the MoD repeatedly warned the media to get out of Baghdad. Yet for the media it is an essential and legitimate part of bearing witness to events – which we believe to be our primary task. Our job is eyewitness reporting, which means being there. The BBC stayed in Saigon as it fell, why shouldn't we stay in Baghdad?

Behind Enemy Lines
This element in covering a war is perhaps the most contentious. The usual argument put forward against media reporting from behind enemy lines is that of 'moral equivalence' – that we improperly equate the justness of the enemy's cause with that of the allied cause.

It's an argument I find hard to accept. I don't believe anyone believed the Iraqi information minister on the roof of the hotel denying the city was falling as American shelling and troops could be heard in the background. And I think the tapes of Osama Bin Laden broadcast by Al Jazeera did more to convince people of his guilt than persuade them of his case. Those who suggest our reporting from behind the lines produces a moral equivalence are perhaps themselves guilty of two things: a disrespect for the intelligence of the public and a lack of confidence in their own case, if they believe it can be so easily undermined.

The second argument against the media being behind enemy lines is that we are unable to operate freely and therefore our reporting is contaminated. We're hardly unaware of the issue. But the same is true of the embedded correspondents and in both cases the reality of restrictions on our reporting were far less than assumed. Rageh Omaar's Iraqi minder spent more time discussing which days off he could take, than preventing us broadcasting. Hardly the iron hand of repression.

And where we were unable to operate freely, we said so. Clarity and transparency with the audience – respect for them and their right to know – is what's vital here.

The BBC has an international reputation as an impartial objective broadcaster. Reporting only one perspective and one point of view won't perpetuate that – it would only undermine our credibility. The BBC Arabic service provided a lifeline of trusted information to the Iraqi people whilst at the same time the coalition forces were tuning into the World Service on the battlefield as they advanced on Baghdad. Good journalism depends on eyewitness reporting. The human nature of journalism means that being there matters. Wars at a distance are not an option for us as they may one day be for the military.

Overview

The final element in the jigsaw of war coverage is the overview, which is usually provided by a defence or diplomatic correspondent or, of course, an armchair general. Centcom in Doha was meant to provide the overview of the Iraq war, which is why the BBC based its defence correspondents there. It didn't work. There were really two different briefing operations going on there.

First, the American operation, which gave precious little away. Indeed the US military spokesman Jim Wilkinson has been explicit, saying the embedded reporters were meant to be the font of all news, not Centcom. There were daily frustrations at the emptiness of the US briefings. One American reporter, Michael Wolf, asked at the press conference: 'Why should we stay? What's the value for us of what we are learning at this million dollar press centre ?' He was of course brought into line and told, 'no more questions'.

Fortunately there was also the British briefing operation with Simon Wren and Al Lockwood. They were more open, sensible and understood the media's needs. However, Centcom appeared unable to cope with the speed of information from the front line onto the air. There is a need to brief in real time. To be able to show what is happening across the campaign. We know the technology to do that exists, but it's not shared.

From my perspective, Centcom fell a long way short of what a twenty-four hour news operation requires. So we fell back on correspondents in London – like Mark Urban on Newsnight and the World at One, or Brian Hanrahan, and of course on those armchair generals. People we hope have experience and understanding of war and who can help us put some perspective on events. They reflect the anxiety and speculation in the country – tempered, we hope, with some expertise.

So, in sum, we had vivid snapshots from the front line, very little independent reporting, journalists in Baghdad under great pressure both from the regime and their own governments, and a central briefing operation which was inadequate, leading us to fall back on whatever expertise we could find in London to present the big picture. To state the obvious, these were very far from perfect circumstances. Moreover, everything we broadcast was scrutinized and criticized by a deeply divided public.

Tenor of War Coverage

The BBC was accused of being both too negative and of being a government mouthpiece, and also of being inconsistent in our judgement about how well the war was progressing. But it wasn't just us. As Donald Rumsfeld said on 28 March:

> *We have seen mood swings in the media from highs to lows to highs and back again sometimes in a single twenty-four hour period. For some the massive volume of television and the breathless reports can seem somewhat disorientating.*

Critics say that a relentless scepticism, an appetite for playing devil's advocate, inexperienced presenters and a focus on unlikely scenarios displaced proper analysis.

I believe, rather, that we reflected what we heard and what we were told, and the way the military, the government and the country were feeling about the war.

Before the conflict we reported many of the briefings which anticipated a rapid and easy victory ('a cakewalk'). Expectations were deliberately raised.

When troops encountered stiffer than expected resistance we reported that too. When some military officers expressed concern about the strategy and progress we reported that. We didn't make it up. Officers on the battlefield told us of their anxieties. Andrew Tyndall, who analyzes TV News in the US, was indignant:

Rumsfeld has a lot of nerve. Pentagon officials inflated expectations of a quick surrender by Iraqis as part of their pre-war propaganda knowing journalists would repeat those claims. Then they turn around and complain about mood swings when the statements they knew were not true turn out not to be.

Military propaganda is, of course, entirely legitimate. It helps win wars. Sir Terence Lewin, Chief of the Defence Staff at the time of the

Falklands, observed:

> I do not see it as deceiving the press or the public. I see it as deceiving the enemy. Anything I can do to help me win is fair as far as I'm concerned.

It would be naive to suppose otherwise. But the media's role is not to be complicit. We have to retain the trust of the audience – which is increasingly global for everything the BBC broadcasts – especially when it is deeply divided, as the domestic audience was in the case of the Iraq war.

The BBC spends a lot of time trying to cut through spin and manipulation, trying to find out what else is happening besides the 'message of the day'. And we are naturally hostile to being used. This puts media and military inevitably at odds. But it also places us more firmly than ever in the same bed – the presentation of war to a global public. Herein the media raises questions of justification and accountability and the military seeks to pre-empt them or present firm answers. Prof Philip Taylor from Leeds University, who has written more perceptively on this than most, wrote in the *Washington Post*:

> The contemporary catchphrase for propaganda is 'perception management.' An ugly phrase, it is the product of an MBA-influenced belief that wars can be packaged in the style of a marketing or advertising campaign. It is based on the idea that war, or any policy, can be 'sold' like a product. After 9/11, there may not have been much need to market war in the United States, but the concept appears not to be working quite so well with more critical target audiences: Iraqis, the Muslim world generally and, most disconcertingly, the United States' NATO allies in Europe.

And this is where I believe 'perception management' still has a long way to go. In the United States, still traumatized by 11 September, they feel themselves to be at war and dissent is little tolerated. The media, by and large, have fallen into line.

Seminal Changes in Media and Reporting

Europe, and much of the rest of the world, does not feel itself to be at war. And the values of democratic debate with a diversity of views are held high. And global media, much of which will resist the packaging of war, is developing at an ever faster rate. Twenty-four hour news channels, with which we have hardly come to terms and which still produce the editorial pressures noted above, are already out of date. There is now a new media, with new journalists producing new news, who have little regard for those of us in the traditional media. With a laptop and a phone connection websites can 'broadcast' from anywhere, unregulated. *The Guardian* ran the 'Web log' of an unknown man in Baghdad reporting his daily diary from the city under attack; there was a Russian intelligence site offering raw intelligence briefings; there were many dozens of anti-war web sites offering a different perspective and challenging the messages of the coalition on not just a daily but an hourly basis. All this was accessible from anywhere in the world.

Since Kosovo the BBC has received and run mobile phone calls and emails from civilians caught up in war. Now those civilians are running their own coverage of events. It's not just Al Jazeera that offers a different point of view. With a satellite dish you can sit at home and watch dozens of channels from all over the world and receive the raw material being beamed into newsrooms before public transmission. The genie is now out of the bottle and won't go back.

Military planners have been slow to keep up with changes in the journalistic profession, often applying the lessons of the last conflict to the next one. That may not work any more. In short, military information planning has only just come to terms with the twenty-four hour news cycle. But the media has taken another quantum leap.

What are the implications of this? For starters, there will be a lot more information out there. Controlling it all will be impossible. But making sense of it will be much harder too. The message of the war now has a global audience, not just a domestic one. That makes it very different. Domestic public opinion is but one element of how a conflict will be judged. World opinion is now applying leverage in a way it never has before. And in this context the doctrine of 'You're either with us or against us' is counter-productive. Al Jazeera may not reflect Western tastes, but for its Arab audience it is a strong and legitimate journalistic voice. To deny that will be to lose a key constituency in world opinion.

Furthermore, there will be not just a few, not just dozens, but many hundreds of channels of communication with a great diversity of views. They won't all fall into line. They will question and test the picture presented and offer contrary views. That's a challenge to conventional media as much as for governments and the military. This places a greater premium than ever on credibility and integrity of the message for both the military and the media. Trust becomes the key. Yet the public are trusting governments, military and the media less. That does not mean we should expect the whole truth to always be told, especially where operational security and troops' safety are at stake. But it does mean the truth will be tested – hence the current debate about Weapons of Mass Destruction. Prof Taylor again:

> *No one party – not the coalition, not the Iraqis, not the anti-war campaigners, nor the journalists (whether embedded or not) – has a monopoly on the truth. That would be incredible. But democratic governments, if they have the courage of their convictions, should argue what they see as the truth as forcefully and as convincingly as they can, and should be prepared to counter the Truths of their opponents. That is what democracy based on consensus means.*

The old military notion that the media were a problem to be contained and got round is not just wrong. It's now irrelevant: mass, fragmented and uncontrollable media are here to stay.

Whether that's a good or a bad thing is a separate issue. I believe that, in the long run, it's overwhelmingly for the good. It demands openness, and reinforces the values of democratic debate. But it's happened so fast, we have a difficult period of adjustment to go through where the public will assess these multiple global sources, question their traditional sources of information and institutions, and test their credibility before coming to terms with what works for them. As a result, obfuscation, refusal to talk, lies or unreasonable exaggerations – which all lose the trust of the public – will likely become increasingly illegitimate in 'perception management'.

Openness, strong argument, consistency and integrity of the message will be increasingly important to win public trust. And that trust is vital to pursue political or military ends. Can governments or the military working in a political framework always offer that? I don't know. Indeed, will the media, working within the limitations outlined above, be able to offer that? It will be tough. But the price of failure will be a loss of faith by the public in what those of us involved at any point of the triangle (government, military, media) believe to be honourable and important.

Conclusion

The mass of information available will probably mean that most people most of the time will rely on the main news media for their window on the world. The military and the media will remain, as a consequence, mutually dependant in war coverage – the media for access and information, the military for communication with global opinion.

But globalization, media fragmentation, the speed of development of communications technology, and social change mean it's becoming harder and more complicated for governments to win public approval for war. And in the wake of that, the tensions between the media and the military, trying to accommodate each other and their own different imperatives, are going to be considerably greater than in the past. Both the military and the media learn lessons from each conflict and apply them to the next.

I began by asserting that neither governments nor militaries have yet recognized the consequences of war in a wired, globalized, media-rich world. I also noted that while the military want to win, the media want to find out the truth.

Perhaps what the Iraq War will remind us is that truth and trust are a pre-condition of winning.

May 2003, RUSI Whitehall Paper 59

10. Politics and Governance in the New Iraq
Reconstruction of the New Versus Resurrection of the Old

Gareth Stansfield

Gareth Stansfield is Professor of Middle East Politics at the University of Exeter. He is author of *Iraq: People, History, Politics* (2007) and *The Future of Iraq: Dictatorship, Democracy or Division?* (2004).

'An indigenous dynamic has emerged which is characterized by the political resurrection of old socio-political forces, whereby the enduring political and social features of the state are being re-assembled to form a new Iraq.'

The removal of Saddam's dictatorship from its all-pervasive seat of power in Baghdad proved to be a quick and reasonably 'clean' affair for the Coalition of the Willing.[1] However, the clinical removal of Saddam's insidious regime has not been followed by an equally efficient transition of authority and the creation of institutions capable of adequately governing Iraq in an interim period of an undetermined length. Indeed, far from matching the quick and clean 'Part I' of regime change (removing Saddam), 'Part II' (replacing Saddam) promises to be a rather slow affair, punctuated by moments of potentially perilous instability. It would appear that there are contradictory forces in play with regard to the future development of Iraq. On the one hand, there is a US-initiated desire to see political reconstruction, implying that the political structures and mechanics of the Iraqi state are to be created anew. Conversely, an indigenous dynamic has emerged which is characterized by the political resurrection of old socio-political forces, whereby the enduring political and social features of the state are being re-assembled to form a new Iraq.[2]

If the multitude of papers and analyses produced by the US government and associated think-tanks are considered, in addition to the edifice of academic and media speculation that has been generated regarding 'the future of Iraq' it can be seen that 'reconstruction' in its truest form –

(i.e.,) starting anew – was, and remains, a fundamental policy aim of the neo-conservative influenced US administration. The political reconstruction of Iraq, from this perspective, is to build toward a representative system of government, one which enshrines democratic ideals and supports US policy in the Middle East. However, if Iraq in the aftermath of Saddam's removal from power is considered, it is the enduring political and social features of the country that are emergent and, at the present time, these features are tending to have a communal colouring. Eighty-three years of Iraqi history would indicate that this was always a potential possibility. At its formation, Iraq was an artificial creation, encompassing many communal groups with authority radiating from a Sunni Arab dominated Baghdad.[3] Nearly a century of a constant nationalist agenda emanating from successive Iraqi governments, combined with either assimilating patronage or fear-instilling coercion, has partly succeeded in breaking the bonds of communalism and encouraging an 'Iraqi' identity. However, it would seem to be evident that the internal linkages within these groups (whilst they are admittedly internally politically incohesive) are reactivated and solidified during times of heightened tension, and post-Saddam Iraq is certainly one such time.

The Shia community, fragmented though it may be, is realizing the power of its popularist muscles, and the religious establishment is coming to terms with the inherent political power a Shia communal identity could release if harnessed effectively. The Kurds in the north are, rather shockingly for the Arabs, perhaps the elder statesmen of this new Iraq with their decade-long autonomous political development behind them, and with the most coherent and unified political strategy of any political, or communal, group. With regard to more traditional groups which may possess a cross-communal identity, the tribes, once dismissed as being irrelevant in understanding the politics of urbane Iraq, are now resurgent. The most obvious example of this is the empowerment of a local tribal head by the British forces in Basra, but there are several examples of tribal groups becoming politically involved in other areas, including Kut and Najaf. The Sunni Arabs, perhaps in a state of shock after the rapid demise of Saddam, are more noticeable by their silence rather than any overt political activity. Yet they remain pre-eminent in a political sense due to the history and culture of Iraq, but also due to the fact that they are still the most wealthy component of society, unified in their Arab orientation and Iraqi fear of Iranian encroachment into their affairs (a fear, incidentally, that is shared by many of their Shia countrymen) and, now, Kurdish developments in the north including the brief occupation of Kirkuk and Mosul. The much-vaunted US policy of 'de-Ba'athification' is a further threat to the traditional Sunni-dominated elites who, with some justification, presume that attempts to rid Iraq of the cancer of the Ba'ath party would effectively turn into a Sunni witch-hunt of McCarthy-esque type proportions. Faced with such external pressures, one may expect that most powerful of the enduring trends of Iraqi politics to manifest itself in the near future – Sunni Arab political organization and subsequent association with, and political dominance of, the institutions of state.

This is therefore the crux of what may be an intractable problem. The US usage of phrases such as 'the reconstruction of Iraq' and 'the rebuilding of Iraq' are not accidental. They belie a deep ideological desire originating within the administration to reconstruct Iraq politically – to start anew with fresh non-Ba'athist institutions of government, with an electorate focused toward a secular agenda concomitant with a political outlook of acceptance toward US involvement in its affairs (including economic) and matched by a cathartic embrace of the legitimacy of the state of Israel. This external policy drive is being challenged by Iraq's enduring internal political characteristics – distinctive nationalist tendencies, anti-imperialism and a strong antipathy toward Israel, a kaleidoscopic political society with multiple poles of authority, powerful confessional tendencies and historical legacies of regime-driven association, oppression, benevolence and rivalry which may prove impossible to resolve, let alone remove. It is this battle of reconstruction from on high versus the reconsolidating nature of political resurrection from below, enacted on the proverbial chessboard of Iraq and manipulated by a cornucopia of internal, regional, international and transnational interests, which promises to ensure that the future political development of Iraq has the potential to be a tortuous experience for all concerned.

With such a division in mind, it is a useful exercise to develop an analysis which addresses the forces behind the external 'reconstruction' agenda, and the internal 'resurrection' process. Of course, both are complex, and the division is somewhat of an arbitrary nature, but it is illuminating to glimpse in the briefest of terms the dynamics which are claiming to be acting in the interests of the new Iraq, and those which have been reborn in the newly unfettered, though rather unstable, post-Saddam political climate. It would appear that for the future of Iraq to be deemed satisfactory by all involved in the undertaking of regime change, from the viewpoint of the immediate post-Saddam setting, an infinitesimally narrow path has to be found which satisfies the aims of US policy-makers, whilst pacifying the burgeoning, powerful, political forces of Iraq and, indeed, the greater Middle East region and Islamic world.

Toward Reconstruction of the New

In the eyes of the ultra-right of the US political spectrum, the issue is not only about the reconstruction of Iraq, it is about reconstructing the Middle East. This group, often termed the 'neo-conservatives', includes the so called 'hawks' of the administration, Vice-President Dick Cheney, Deputy Secretary for Defense Paul Wolfowitz, the former director of the CIA James Woolsey, and the irrepressible Richard Perle. These are merely the most prominent figures in a powerful and influential association of individuals and organizations.[4] The neo-con agenda has its roots in the mid-1950s with leftist intellectuals angered by the inability of the US to confront Soviet aggression. Their transformation into a right-wing collection of intellectuals came resplendent with an evangelical belief in the values of political democracy and economic liberalism, albeit in the style of US institutions and methods. Kept on the fringes of political activity, even with Republicans in power, 11 September 2001 brought their ideological descendants to centre-stage, along with their radical agenda for changing the political structure of the Middle East out of all recognition. The continued survival of Saddam's Iraq was an obvious, and seemingly easy, starting point. The idea of reconstructing Iraq in such a way that it would be a 'new Iraq', one which would be home to a 'Western' style democracy, complete with the associated and necessary range of institutions of civil society has been a common theme in literature associated with Iraq since the drive toward regime change became apparent. Fuelled by the sentiments of the neo-conservative dominated White House, Iraq became identified as a 'strategic prize' and its democratic transformation would act as the catalyst that proactively encourages democratic change in the entire Middle East region.

Since October 2001 in particular, the neo-cons were assembling the tools by which Iraq would be reconstructed. The most important component of these plans was to ensure that the future administration of Iraq would be headed, or at least dominated, by a figure and group in which the US could be confident that it had influence over, and would act in the interests of the US in the region. Dr Ahmed Chalabi and the Iraqi National Congress (INC) fitted the bill admirably. Chalabi, with his association with the Republicans going back to 1990, was given a running start in the post-Saddam Iraq by being airlifted by the Pentagon at an early point into Nasiriya, and it would be a mistake to underestimate the power and scope of plans of the right-wing of US politics, and particularly Wolfowitz and Perle, to place Chalabi in a position of influence in a new Iraqi state. Chalabi's placement in Nasiriya with Pentagon active support along with his commanding of the Free Iraqi Forces (FIF) presents an attempt to secure a *fait accompli* for the neo-cons.

Irrespective of whatever grand democratic plan exists for Iraq, the US still had to move quickly after Saddam's regime collapsed in an attempt to prevent the country descending into widepread anarchy. General Jay Garner, a figure associated strongly with the neo-conservatives of the Pentagon, arrived in Baghdad on 21 April, with the task of restoring basic services to Iraq as soon as possible. Garner's Pentagon-supported Office of Reconstruction and Humanitarian Assistance (ORHA) entered Iraq in order to bring some semblance of authority to a very unstable situation, and to provide immediate humanitarian relief and facilitate the restarting of vital services. However, he had been beaten to it by the Shia religious establishment, and by enterprising (if slightly dubious) individuals such as Mohammad Mohsen Zubaidi – the self-proclaimed 'Mayor of Baghdad' until his unceremonious arrest by US forces at the end of April.[5] The ORHA also ran into serious difficulties in identifying who should be empowered and employed from the local community. The problem of identifying and verifying figures associated with the previous Ba'ath regime proved to be an insurmountable task, and the ORHA was forced into either being seen as supporting ex-Ba'athists to return to work as policemen, for example, or to allow the presence of localized militia forces to assist in establishing law and order. The role of the US, and particularly that of General Garner and his successors, in Iraq is often compared to that of the US and General Douglas MacArthur in Japan.[6] *The Economist* noted that whether the occupiers of Iraq are mourned upon their leaving, as happened in Japan, will depend on how good a job they do at rebuilding. However, Iraq 2003 is not Japan 1945. Although the political slate was certainly not 'clean' in Japan, it was somewhat more easy for the US to operate in post-war environment in a Japan devastated by the economic and military impacts of world war, beaten into fearful submission by the use of atomic weapons, and forced into humiliating and humbling defeat, symbolized by the highly public surrender of Emperor Hirohito. Arguably, Iraq will not be so 'easy' and the end result far less pliant.

Attempts to secure a US-style reconstruction of Iraq are being dashed by two related variables – one is the Iraqi people themselves, and the second is the opposition from the State Department and the National Security Council (NSC) toward the domineering activities of the neo-con Pentagon. Arguably, it is this infighting in Washington DC that is giving opportunities for other regional powers to promote their own candidates for office, whilst simultaneously weakening the unity of the established exiled opposition.[7] Indeed, the fact that these arguments are still vociferously and ferociously being played out would suggest that the actual detailed planning of reconstructing Iraq on the ground has remained woefully inadequate. The meetings which occurred at Nasiriya (15 April) and Baghdad (28 April) were attempts by the more liberal components of the US administration to encourage a political leadership to emerge from within Iraq, thereby weakening the committee elected at the Pentagon-sponsored meetings, dominated by the exiled opposition, in Salahadin (Kurdistan) in March. At this meeting, a six-man committee was elected from the leaders of the Iraqi opposition, which comprised Chalabi, Massoud Barzani (KDP), Jalal Talabani (PUK), Ayatollah Mohammad Bakr al-Hakim (SCIRI), Iyad Allawi (INA) and Adnan Pachachi (independent). Allawi and Pachachi later withdrew, leaving Chalabi pre-eminent in the committee as the one figure the US could deal with regarding the future of the whole of Iraq.[8] The next conference, planned for the end of May, will perhaps see which US policy line is winning.

Toward Resurrection of the Old
The rebirth of the forces of the 'old Iraq' has been traumatic as different groups backed by, at times, opposing powers are thrust into the political arena. Exiled organizations and figures who have publicly fought for the removal of Saddam and the imposition of their idea of a new Iraq with

the support of regional and interested states now have to find a place in the political landscape of the post-Saddam Iraq, alongside leaders of groups arising from inside Iraq itself who understandably enjoy higher levels of popular legitimacy. The ensuing *mêlée* as these radically different entities compete for the prize of dominance in the future Iraq perhaps has more chance of promoting instability and the potential fragmenting of Iraqi political society rather than enhancing internal security and the cohesion of the state. Again, at whatever level of analysis one chooses to view recent events in the post-Saddam Iraq, the use of the 'external' reconstruction versus 'internal' resurrection framework can explain to some extent the rapidly increasing tension accumulating in the political system.

Perhaps the greatest example of the perverse impact the implementation of an external reconstructionist policy is having is upon the primordialization of Iraqi society. Whilst not discounting communal identities, academics consistently have argued that the depiction of Iraq as the Kurdish north, the Sunni Arab 'centre' and the Shia (and therefore Iran-friendly) Arab south is so reductionist that it is perhaps misleading. These groups are thoroughly mixed, their boundaries are changeable and at times ambiguous, and inter-communal groups are also prominent. One only has to highlight the most basic overlap as being Kurdish Sunnis, Sunni Arabs, Arab Shia, Shia Kurds to understand that it is not a straightforward task to start drawing lines on maps, and the reality on the ground is far more complicated than even this rather confusing overlap portrays. However, coalition actions are heralding the institutionalization of this three-way model. The ORHA itself envisages the division of Iraq, in the short term at least, into a northern component administered from Mosul, a centre administered from Baghdad, and a southern component administered from Basra. If this conforms to any historical model, it is to that of the Ottoman Empire's division of the region into the *vilayets* of Mosul, Baghdad and Basra, and not to any brave new conception of post conflict administration. Arguably, left to its own devices, the Iraqi population, complete with its myriad complexities, would find a political solution to its problem of governance and representation which fits the characteristics of Iraqi society. However, a three-way neo-*vilayet* division imposed in the interests of executing emergency government may act as a catalyst in igniting the forces which seek to break the artificial state's cohesion into its base communal components. Whatever the exponents of the complexity of Iraqi society theories may say, Iraq is now clearly, at least at this moment in time, divided into distinct communal groups which are undergoing a process of coalescing their internal political forces. This is, perhaps, an understandable reaction after living under a repressive regime for decades whereby no cultural identity apart from that of Iraqi (Ba'athi) nationalism was encouraged. However, this temporary political rebound to communal identity could easily be made permanent by ill considered short-term policies which have dire long-term consequences.

A key problem facing the reconstructionists is exactly how they can translate the policies designed in the security of the neo-conservative domains in the US into reality on the ground. Indeed, with regard to constructing a 'new Iraq', the devil is very much in the detail. It is a relatively easy task (even though there was a great amount of bickering) to organize meetings and to draft the thirteen points agreed at Nasiriya (which were so basic that they could have been drafted by any collection of Iraqi individuals), and to agree to meet again in Baghdad. Where the problem seems to lie with any gathering of Iraqi political forces meeting under the auspices of the coalition is that few tangible policies or concrete positions which could have a profound impact upon Iraq are forwarded, let alone adopted. Perhaps it is a problem of political legitimacy. The groups which are will ing to claim popular legitimacy, such as affiliates of the Shia religious establishment, either do not attend the meetings in order not to offend their followers or sponsors, or if they do attend (such as SCIRI) are treated with a certain amount of trepidation by the US. Even Chalabi and the INC are not willing publicly to adopt a position of leadership in this most volatile of times. The initial and perhaps greatest problem facing those on the ground is that the forces and entities which were presupposed to exist in Iraq, or to act in a manner predicted previously to support the drive toward reconstruction, have not yet materialized. With the removal of Saddam, it would seem to be the case that few, if any, leaders have emerged from the masses of Iraqi society who conform to what the regime change planners were expecting. The resurrection of the authority of the Shia religious establishment, for example, has been effective and widespread, both in the south and in Baghdad. The *Financial Times* noted on 25 April that 'while the US is only now setting up the new Iraqi interim administration, the [Shia] clerics have been working the ground quietly, without fanfare'.[9] Indeed, whatever path the Coalition forces of political reconstruction seem to tread, they are following in the footsteps of the resurrected forces of the old socio-political groups.

This leads to further problems, which if not resolved quickly will prove to be a threat to the future security of Iraq. Of immediate concern is the open availability of large numbers and types of weapons, combined with the political free-for-all which is in danger of developing.[10] All groups, irrespective of their position in the range of reconstructionist entities or forces of indigenous resurrection, have an immediate interest in creating armed militia and enhancing their military power. The Kurds, interestingly, for the first time in the Iraqi state have the most organized standing military force, far more sizeable and capable than any other military formation in Iraq at present, apart from that of the US. In their dogged quest to secure Kurdish rights in the new Iraq, and faced with worrying expressions of Arab nationalism and Islamic religious sentiment (which Kurds presume to mean anti-democratic) along with the omnipresent threat of Turkish military action against the north of Iraq, it is understandable that the principle Kurdish parties are wisely cautious in standing down their combined force of approximately 80,000 *peshmerga*.[11] However, the Kurdish issue in Iraq is one which is secondary in the current reconstruction debate, unless, of course, Turkey was to embark on a military escapade into northern Iraq. Perhaps of more immediate concern is the mushrooming presence of armed militias in the centre and south of the country. Alongside the traditional militia forces of tribal groups and powerful families (and the military strength of some of these tribes should not be underestimated), there is now underway an expansion of militia forces associated with either US-led policies, or indigenous Iraqi political groups.

The most notable of the new militia groups to have appeared in the post-Saddam Iraq are the Free Iraqi Forces (FIF), which is the newly formed armed wing of the INC. The FIF dresses in US supplied uniforms, and reportedly operates closely with coalition forces. The Shia SCIRI has the *Badr* Brigade, and there are several other groups in Iraq now emerging which have access to arms, whilst displaying loyalty to different sectarian leaderships. Indeed, the US army has gone as far as to empower the *Mujahidin al-Khalq* organization (MKO) to act as security guards on the Kirkuk-Baghdad road. Previously identified by the US itself as being a terrorist organization, and implicated with the slaughter of Kurdish villagers in 1991, the MKO has perhaps been resurrected due to its anti-Iranian position, more than the position it occupies within Iraqi society – as a group composed almost entirely of Iranian dissidents, it has no position within any conception of a new Iraq.

The Shia Powerhouse

Before the military attacks against Saddam were ordered, the fact that Iraq is predominantly a Shia country was used with great effect by the press officers of the White House and Whitehall to emphasize the dictatorial and repressive nature of Saddam's regime whereby, according to their reading of history, the Shia were a dispossessed and brutalized majority population living under an authoritarian and chauvinistic Sunni dominated government. The rather naïve belief following from this was that the Shia would choose to fit neatly into a new secular government in which all of Iraq's ethnic and religious groups would be represented. With Saddam's removal, it would appear that the political strength of the Shia religious establishment was grossly underestimated in the pre-war planning stage.[12] Paul Wolfowitz illustrated clearly this belief within the administration when, in early March 2003, he described Iraqis as being secular and 'overwhelmingly Shia', contending that dealing with Iraqis would not bring with it the same problems of dealing with Saudis combined with the sensitivity of Islamic holy places existing on the peninsula. Wolfowitz was correct in the fact that Iraqis are overwhelmingly Shia, but failed to appreciate the power of the religious organizations, and seemed to be oblivious to the importance of the shrine cities of Karbala and Najaf. In fitting with the reconstruction versus resurrection framework, Juan Cole mockingly notes that 'the neo-conservative fantasy of Iraq is now meeting the real Iraq, on the ground, in the shrine cities as well as in the smaller, mostly Shiite towns in the south of the country.'[13]

The sudden removal of Saddam's regime and his apparatus of control from the centre and south of Iraq lifted the shackles of restraint from the Iraqi Shia religious establishment (the *hawza*) which had survived by adopting a strategy of political muteness after the systematic targeting of its members by the security forces of Saddam. Why Saddam feared the Shia *hawza* is a useful question for US policy-makers to address, as they are faced with a resurgent Shia Islamist popular sentiment which apparently was unexpected before the event. Saddam feared the Shia not because they were not Sunnis, nor was he overly concerned about the oft-reported Iranian influence over the *hawza*. After all, Iraqi Shia are firstly Iraqi, and then Shia, and nationalist and secular tendencies remain the most identifying feature of the Iraqi population of the centre and south. The *hawza* hardly ever presented Saddam with a credible threat to his own authority, mainly due to the fact that the leaders of the *hawza* (the *marja'*) did not share in the belief of their Iranian co-religionists' linkage between religion and politics and developed a more spiritual rather than political philosophy regarding the role of Islam in the state. Saddam's fear was neither the *hawza*, nor the Shia *per se*, but the potential for both together to initiate mass political activity which was not in the interests of the regime, and to propagate its effects to the rest of the country in a show of popular strength. Of course, whilst neither the *hawza* nor the secular Shia masses were a threat to the regime whilst they were divided, it was a different matter when a figure or organization bridged the gap and succeeded in politicizing the *hawza*, and spiritualizing the masses. The most significant of these figures was Ayatollah Mohammad Baqir al-Hakim, the inspiriational *marja'* whose allying of the sacred with the political combined with his association with the popular *Hizb al-Da'wa al-Islamiyya* (The Party of the Islamic Call – *Al-Da'wa*) singled him out for execution by the regime in the early 1980s, and led to a wave of oppression against the forces of political Shiism ever since.

Under this repression, *Al-Da'wa* was forced to operate clandestinely, whilst the emasculated *hawza* returned to its core belief of the division between religion and politics.[14] However, Saddam's sensitivity toward any potential figure who could bridge the gap between religion and politics remained keen, and another member of the al-Sadr family, Ayatollah Mohammad Sadiq al-Sadr, was assassinated in Najaf in 1999 after daring to defy the regime. Since 1999, the leading cleric in Iraq has been Grand Ayatollah Ali Sistani of Najaf. Of Iranian origin but of Najaf clerical training, Ayatollah Sistani returned to his Najafi theological roots and preached the separation of religion and politics, allowing Saddam again to make inroads into the secularization of the Shia masses primarily through the organization of the Ba'ath Party. After the removal of Saddam and the occupation of Iraq by coalition forces, Sistani's line has been one of non-interference with US actions, but making his position clear that the extended presence of US forces would be an unwelcome development.[15] Often seen as ineffectual by outside observers, Sistani has a figurehead position amongst the Iraqi Shia, and his pre-eminence as the most important *marja'* within the Najaf *hawza* is acknowledged but, as an Iraqi Ayatollah grounded in the belief of a non-political *hawza*, it is unlikely that Sistani would ever willingly adopt a bridging position linking the *hawza* with the masses.

It is perhaps to be expected that another member of the al-Sadr family would rise to the challenge of merging religion with politics. Following the death of Mohammad Sadiq al-Sadr in 1999 his son, Muqtada al-Sadr, went underground. Over the next three years, Muqtada continued with covert attempts to organize Shia militia in Najaf and Kufa and succeeded in establishing and enhancing his following in the Saddam City quarter of Baghdad. Muqtada al-Sadr's movement (*Jimaat al-Sadr al-Thani*) appears to be authoritarian in nature, and set upon legitimizing the authority of the young al-Sadr (he is reportedly no more than thirty years old) by insisting that only the directives of his deceased father are legitimate, and the clerics of Iranian origin, presumable including Sistani, have no authority in Iraq.[16] Muqtada's brief political career has been notable both in its civil achievements, and association with intimidating violence. He has benefited strongly by having Saddam City as his support base. Renamed *Medinat al-Sadr* (Sadr City), this deprived neighbourhood which includes at least two million people of mainly Shia background is now effectively a zone patrolled by al-Sadr's men, with popular support clearly also in his favour, perhaps due to al-Sadr's establishing a rudimentary support network for the health infrastructure of the city, weeks before General Garner's men arrived. However, this benevolent attitude toward social improvement appears to be matched by a ruthless streak toward potential opponents.

Perhaps the only member of the Shia religious establishment to enjoy the support of western governments, Abdul Majid al-Khoei was tasked with playing a prominent role in the reconstruction of Iraq. The son of the late Grand Ayatollah Abu al-Qasim al-Khoei, he was brought into Iraq on 3 April by US forces, keen to bring the southern cities under some form of pro-US control. In his quest to unite Shia groups in Najaf, he was brutally killed on 10 April as he attempted to reconcile local religious leaders with the Guardian of the Shrine of Ali, Haidar Rifeii al-

Qalidar, fell into chaos. Al-Khoei was stabbed at least thirty times and 'his remains were dragged across the city, leaving a trail of blood on the streets'.[17]

The involvement of Muqtada in the killing of al-Khoei is generally acknowledged as fact, and even if his followers did not do it, he later used the killing to intensify the pressure he was applying against Sistani who he views as being complicit with the atrocities of Saddam's regime by refusing to take a political role against him. Muqtada also threatened Ayatollah Said al-Hakim, the nephew of Ayatollah Mohammad Bakr al-Hakim, leader of the Iran-backed SCIRI. Muqtada's targeting of a group with acknowledged links to Tehran illustrates the division which exists between those pursuing an 'Iraq only' solution, and those who have engendered support from Iran.[18] In political terms, SCIRI was powerful as long as Saddam remained in power, as its support from Tehran and its external base allowed it to occupy a position of leadership, whilst those groups which remained in Iraq, including *Al-Da'wa* and Muqtada's faction were poor, oppressed and seemingly eradicated.[19] However, with Saddam removed, it is the latter groups which are making the headway in the new political realities of Iraq, whilst SCIRI is struggling to gain a popular mandate.

SCIRI's struggle has been a long one. Formed in 1982 in Tehran after Saddam's efficient use of persecution to remove Shia political leaders, SCIRI's leadership has remained close to the hardliners of Iran under the guidance of Ayatollah Ali Khamenei. This association, along with SCIRI's heightened involvement with other Iraqi opposition groups (including the INC) at US sponsored events, has done little to endear it to the Shia public. However, with what is perhaps the most powerful military force available to any Shia group (the *Badr* Brigade)[20] and the support of Tehran, the current period may be difficult for al-Hakim, but he retains a position of considerable influence in Iraq, and it was his call on 18 April for all Shias to undertake the pilgrimage to the Shrine of Hussein in Karbala which resulted in the TV footage guaranteed to drive fear into the hearts of US policymakers – mass demonstrations of a reportedly Islamist hue taking place in the middle of Iraq, with no way of exercising any control over them. The fact that the slogans commonly chanted by the participants were distinctly anti-US occupation rather than particularly Islamic in their tone indicate clearly what Saddam had feared, and what the US has inherited — the power of the Shia *hawza* to mobilize secular sentiment with an Islamic colouring against anybody attempting to rule over them from Baghdad.

The Autonomous Kurds?

On the surface, it seems, the Kurdish experience of regime change has been of a reasonably straightforward nature. Even the supposed problems of the Kurdish occupation of Kirkuk have seemingly melted into insignificance.[21] However, as usual with the Kurds, the reality of the situation would appear to be far more complex and uncertain. The position of the Kurds in Iraq was used to devastating effect by the US pro-war machine. Saddam's gassing of the Kurds in 1988 was used as gruesome evidence of the brutality of the regime and the threat that his possessing of chemical weapons in 1988 transmuted itself into a threat-in-linkage with international terrorism in 2002. The fact that the Kurds had been highlighting Saddam's proven usage of chemical weapons in 1988 was conveniently ignored. This, in many respects, is indicative of the unfortunate Kurdish position in Iraq – when it is useful to highlight their plight and their suffering at the hands of a dictator that is deemed in need of removal, their tragedy is exploited. When it is necessary to support the Iraqi government, as in 1988, the massacre of the Kurds is ignored. It almost seemed that proof of Saddam's WMD programme in 2002 was based upon his usage of chemical weapons in 1988, and images of poisoned civilians in the Kurdish town of Halabja were used by the Coalition to bring a human face to the potential devastation such weapons can inflict. Whether or not Saddam had WMD in 2002, the use of the Kurds gave a moral imperative to the regime change policy. It is a worrying thought that the removal of Saddam may change little how the Kurds are used as victims and abused as subversives in the future.

However, times are now different. The Kurds are no longer the people of the hills, content with their lives on the pastures, willing to live a semi-nomadic life of subsistence farming. They are now an urbanized people, benefiting from the impact of modernity on their lives and, most importantly, they have achieved a degree of political recognition and acceptance by the international community. Since 1991, the Kurds have governed and administered their own region in Iraqi Kurdistan and, since 1997, have refrained from partaking in that most favoured Kurdish past time of internecine bloodletting to present to the democratic world a political system which, whilst having (and, to their credit, admitted) obvious weaknesses, is a significant step forward when compared to what the rest of Iraq had to endure.[22] Regional elections were held in 1992, convening the Kurdistan National Assembly in Erbil. A regional government was formed, which subsequently divided due to the civil war between the KDP and PUK, but Kurdish administration in the north has remained the standard for the 1990s into the 2000s and has perhaps become an institutionalized political feature on the map of the Middle East .

The Kurdish leaders, primarily Barzani and Talabani, have their concerns. *De facto* Iraqi Kurdistan is now a relative success story but the reasons for its success and survival perversely stem from the nemesis of Halabja – Saddam Hussein himself. It was Saddam's voluntary withdrawal from the north in 1991 (an undertaking he had little option to do as he had far more pressing concerns of securing Baghdad), combined with the sanctions regime targeting his military potency which gave the Kurds a modicum of security in their *de facto* state. It may even be considered to have been a symbiotic relationship, as Saddam's need to smuggle oil was met with Kurdish complicity in facilitating trade with Turkey, granting a significant revenue-generating capability to the rather peculiar entity. Existing in a geopolitical anomaly, kept in place by the restraints imposed on Baghdad and Saddam's tactics of dodging them, Iraqi Kurdistan thrived and prospered toward the end of the 1990s. With Saddam removed, the danger is that the anomaly reverts back to the *status quo ante*, and the Kurds have to find their place once again in the new Iraq.

The pitfalls in attempting to manage the political reconstruction of Iraq with regard to the Kurds are legion. The Kurds, quite understandably, desire to maintain their gains and to ensure that they are never again left to the mercy of a dictator with occasional genocidal lapses. For the Kurds, this means a degree of self-government, an influential role in the affairs of Iraq, and the involvement of the international community (and particularly the US) as the ultimate protectors of their freedoms. On paper, it sounds as though this would be the easiest public relations 'sell' of a policy for the US administration. However, the political realities of the Middle East region shine through and threaten to thwart Kurdish aspirations. Turkey, primarily, has serious misgivings about any form of Kurdish autonomy in the north of Iraq, because of the potential example a successful Iraqi Kurdish entity would be to their own Kurds.[23] If this serious external problem was not enough to keep Talabani and Barzani occupied, the internal dimensions of Iraqi politics are perhaps even more menacing. It is a contentious point, but Iraqi Arab public opinion, Shia and Sunni alike, consider Iraq to be an Arab state, as do the majority of other Arab Middle East states.[24] The positioning of Kurdistan in the sensitive northern border regions, along with the incessant Kurdish claim to the important oil-city of Kirkuk, would suggest that any future Arab-dominated Iraqi government would fall into disagreement with the Kurds over the devolution of power at a very early moment in the history of the new Iraq.

The liberation of Kirkuk, ostensibly by Kurdish civilians with the assistance of PUK *peshmerga*, and the brief occupation of the city by forces loyal to Talabani sent shock waves throughout Iraqi Arab society.[25] It also was the crowning moment of Kurdish political achievements in the Middle East, let alone just in Iraq. The level of Kurdish pride generated by holding Kirkuk, no matter how briefly, will make any attempt to reduce the current level of Kurdish autonomy in the north a most difficult negotiating exercise. However, what is an issue of pride for the Kurds of Kirkuk is a harbinger of fear for the Arabs and Turkomen of the city. After suffering the hardships of being removed from the city by Saddam's Arabization policies, displaced peoples have returned to Kirkuk to claim what was ancestrally theirs. However, Arab families were in their place and understandably express their unwillingness to leave.[26] In addition to this most serious problem of ownership of territory, the Kurds and the Turkomen both claim a certain dominion over the city which could provoke grievous instability. Indeed, with the clash between Kurds and Turkomen on the one side, and Arabs on the other regarding occupation of land, and a disagreement existing between Kurds and Turkomen regarding the true ethnic balance of the city, Kirkuk has the potential to be Palestine and Sarajevo all rolled into one, with the oil fields fuelling further any decline into conflict unless the external political reconstruction of the city is urgently undertaken by US forces. It is perhaps the one place in Iraq where the implementation of a policy of literal reconstruction can be seen to be truly in the interests of the Iraqi people.[27]

In this immediate aftermath period, the KDP and PUK have followed a most careful and sensible political strategy, apart from their brief excursions into Kirkuk and Mosul. Operating closely alongside US forces, they have done everything possible in order to ensure that Turkey did not have an excuse to enter their region, and have managed to continue to play a predominant role within the Iraqi opposition and in the rounds of meetings hosted by General Garner. However, their problem period is not the current time. The eyes of the world are on Iraq and it is clear that relative peace and tranquility reign supreme in Iraqi Kurdistan, whereas strife and hardship appears to be the norm for the rest of Iraq. The Kurdish desire for a federal Iraq is also known and it would be difficult to envisage a situation in which some form of autonomy for the Kurds is not enshrined in any temporary constitution of an interim authority.[28] However, the problem for the Kurds is further in the future, and particularly over the arguments which appear to be brewing regarding the status of Kirkuk and its oil.[29] When the eyes of the world turn away from Iraq and toward the next international crisis, the Kurds may find that defending their short-term gains made in the early 2000s proves to be more difficult than it was winning them. It is for this reason that the Kurdish parties are aggressively attempting to secure their future in Iraq, through the Iraqi opposition, and by attempting to enshrine federalism as an immoveable reality of a future Iraqi state. Kurds in Iraq therefore constitute a communal group which is fighting to become an institutional reality.[30]

Whither the Sunni?

It should be of note that the direction of discourse regarding the future of Iraq seems to make little note of the situation of the Arab Sunnis, which should be of concern to those dealing with the future of Iraq. To remove the Arab Sunnis from their traditional positions of authority within the state will prove to be a burdensome task for whoever has to do it. Their silence and the lack of any political grouping dominated by them at this point should not be taken as evidence of their political apathy in the future. They have shown a consistent ability to secure unrivalled access to the levers of power in Baghdad, and will not relinquish this historical legacy lightly. Throughout the eighty-three years of Iraq's existence, there has always emerged a core Sunni Arab element who act as the principle actors and guardians of the regime. Arguably, in this regard, Saddam and his Tikritis were little different to King Faisal and his Sharifians. Of course, both relied on foreign support to ensure their survival and ability to maintain their power-base, but it is perhaps a further enduring trend of the Iraqi political construct which may reappear once the political system achieves a state of equilibrium after the recent upheavals. In addition, the desire by neighbouring states to the west and south to ensure Sunni hegemony in Baghdad for reasons pertaining to their own domestic stability should not be underestimated.

Conclusion

It is apparent that the removal of Saddam's regime was comparatively easy compared to its replacement. At whatever scale one considers the political reconstruction of Iraq, the project is complicated by the lack of an agreed idea on what Iraq should 'be'. Every political, communal, and tribal group within the country has a distinct normative position, and the members of the international community are similarly divided. Even within countries of the coalition, the lack of a unified vision – beyond glibly mentioning 'democracy' in a variety of guises – is worryingly evident, the most notable example being the semi-permanent fracture which exists within the US administration regarding the construction and composition of an interim authority. Combined with this, a problem remains of securing international legitimacy for any interim political structure. The battle between US domination of a future authority, or UN mandated responsibility/guidance is only just beginning to gather pace, yet promises to turn into a political struggle of significant magnitude as members of the Security Council, and especially Russia and France, have considerable economic motives to reduce Washington's influence over the design and composition of an interim Iraqi authority.

The reconstructionist agenda versus resurrectionist process is creating palpable tension within Iraq as the US attempts to come to terms with how to implement its democratic strategy in the face of heightening localized political sentiment, often expressed in anti-US occupation tones. Within Iraq, the artificial foundations of the state have been re-opened by the removal of Saddam's government and the lack of any replacement with a domestically legitimated authority. The task of administration is now being devolved by necessity to local groups which have an inherently communal nature and identity. It may be a 'rebound' effect, but, arguably, coalition policy is enforcing age-old divisions within Iraqi society and what may be a temporary resurgence and expression of identity is made into a resilient and possible militant characteristic of the new Iraq. If this is the case, and presuming that the international community would not embrace the managed partition of Iraq into distinct zones (Kurdish and Arab, for example), nor welcome a Shia dominated government with theocratic tendencies, it is a dynamic which may prove difficult to reverse without resorting to Saddam's tried and tested methods of patronage and coercion. Whether the international community, the Coalition, or a future interim administration would be prepared to mimic such policies in the interests of maintaining the territorial integrity of Iraq remains to be seen.

Notes

[1] This chapter benefits from interviews conducted in later April 2003 with Iraqi politicians in London, including Dr Latif Rashid (Patriotic Union of Kurdistan) and Sharif Ali Bin Al-Hussein (Constitutional Monarchy Movement) and other sources who choose to remain anonymous.

[2] The Oxford English Dictionary defines 'reconstruction' as *'to construct anew'* and 'resurrection' as *'restoration to previous status or vogue'*. *Oxford English Dictionary*, 2nd ed., 1989.

[3] See Charles Tripp, *A History of Iraq* (Cambridge: CUP, 2000), p. 45.

[4] For information on the groupings which existed in the US leading up to the invasion of Iraq, see Judith Yaphe, 'America's War on Iraq: Myths and Opportunities', in Toby Dodge & Steven Simon (eds.), 'Iraq at the Crossroads: State and Society in the Shadow of Regime Change', *Adelphi Paper* 354, International Institute for Strategic Studies (Oxford: OUP, 2003), pp. 23-44, quote at p. 25.

[5] See Andrew Buncombe, 'Baghdad's Self-Proclaimed 'Mayor' Promises Islamic Laws', *The Independent*, 21 April 2003.

[6] See 'Special Report: Rebuilding Iraq: The Hard Path to New Nationhood', *The Economist*, April 19-25, 2003, pp. 17-19.

[7] See Gareth Stansfield, 'Toward a New Government in Iraq: Farce of Future?' in *The World Today*, Vol. 59, No. 4 (April). London: Royal Institute of International Affairs, 2003, pp. 7-9; Eli Lake, 'The Bushies Two Plans for Iraq.' *The New Republic Online*, 24 April 2003.

[8] For the US, in dealing with Iraq-proper, the Kurdish leaders remain problematic, as whilst they represent their Kurdish followers, they have no following in Arab Iraq, and the US still baulks at dealing with SCIRI

and its allegedly pro-Iranian orientation.

[9] Roula Khalaf, 'Clerics take charge as generals dither', *Financial Times*, 25 April 2003.

[10] *The Christian Science Monitor* wrote that 'on the Baghdad black market today [25 April] the most casual potential customer can find a Chinese-made AK-47 [assault rifle] for around $25…and 200 rounds of ammunition for a dollar' (Peter Ford, 'Multitude of militias pose threat to democracy in Iraq' *Christian Science Monitor*, , 25 April 2003). Sources within the Iraqi opposition noted to the author that the price for AK-47s had fallen as low as $15.

[11] *Peshmerga* is the Kurdish name for guerrilla.

[12] See Glenn Kessler & Dana Priest, 'US Planners Surprised by Strength of Iraqi Shiites' *The Washington Post*, , 23 April 2003, p. A01.

[13] Juan Cole, 'Shiite Religious Parties Fill Vacuum in Southern Iraq' in *Middle East Report Online*, 22 April 2003.

[14] It was also apparent that the Shia masses were supportive of the Iraqi nationalist agenda during the Iran-Iraq War, choosing to fight against their co-religionists in Iran for the Iraqi state. This is often, and correctly, viewed as evidence of the 'Iraqi' identity of the Iraqi Shia. It is also representative of the division which exists between the Shia and Iran and those of Iraq.

[15] Yaroslav Trofimov, 'Shiite Power Struggle Threatens Stability', *The Wall Street Journal*, 17 April 2003, p. 10.

[16] Hooman Peimani, 'The ever-threatening Shi'ite Factor', *Asia Times*, 18 April 2003.

[17] Trofimov, *Op. cit.*, p. 10.

[18] In the convoluted world of Iraqi politics, a theory exists that Moqtada is a tool of Iranian intelligence, and particularly of the hardliners, who wish to see Sistani and the Najaf *hawza* forced out of the city and relocated to Qum in Iran in a bid to preserve the current leading position of the Iranian city in Shiism in general. Najaf, free to interact with the rest of the Shia community, would soon eclipse all other centres – something which the Iranian hardliners are seeking to prevent by encouraging the activities of Moqtada.

[19] *Al-Da'wa* is perhaps the dark horse of opposition politics. It has been in existence since at least 1958 and, whilst it idolises the figure of the martyred Mohammad Baqir al-Sadr, its leadership has remained collegiate in

structure, and as a party has been divided into different centres of influence within Iraq, and across the Iraqi diaspora. As a party, its support base was consistently the lower middle classes and, once the sensationalism of Muqtada's activities have worn off, it could be expected that *Al-Da'wa* will gain a highly influential position.

[20] Faleh Jabar notes that the *Badr* Brigade remains under the direct command of the Iranian Revolutionary Guard (the *Pasdaran*), again emphasizing the inherent weakness of SCIRI. Faleh Jabar, 'Clerics, Tribes, Ideologues and Urban Dwellers in the South of Iraq: The Potential for Rebellion,' in Dodge & Simon (eds.) *Op. cit.*, pp. 161-178.

[21] See, for example, Gareth Stansfield, "Iraq and its Kurdish State: Dream On' in *The World Today* (Vol. 59, No. 3, February 2003). London: Royal Institute of International Affairs.

[22] For an account of the development of the Iraqi Kurdish *de facto* state, see Gareth Stansfield, *Iraqi Kurdistan: Political Development & Emergent Democracy* (London: RoutledgeCurzon, 2003).

[23] See Graham Fuller, 'Kurds pose a moment of truth for Turkey' *Los Angeles Times*, 21 April 2003.

[24] Interestingly, Libya tends to support the Kurdish aspirations in Iraq.

[25] See Ilene Prusher, 'Top Kurdish Leader Assesses the Costs of War', *Christian Science Monitor*, 16 April 2003.

[26] See May Beth Sheridan, 'Hundreds being ousted as displaced group reclaims land taken over 30 years ago' *Washington Post Foreign Service*, 21 April 2003, p. A15.

[27] See Patrick Cockburn, 'On the plains, Kurds and Arabs clash in the most dangerous flashpoint of all', *The Independent*, 15 April 2003.

[28] See 'Kurdish parliament debates draft constitutions for 'federal' Iraq', AFP, 31 October 2002.

[29] See Daniel Williams & Karl Vick, 'Kurds Redrawing Map by Memory, with Force', *Washington Post Foreign Service*, 17 April 2003, p. A25.

[30] See Gareth Stansfield, 'The Iraqi Kurds: A New Start or Repeated History' *RUSI Newsbrief* (Vol. 23, No. 4, April 2003), pp. 40-41.

May 2003, RUSI Whitehall Paper 59

11. Europe and the United States
An End to Illusions

Jonathan Eyal

Jonathan Eyal is Director of International Security Studies, RUSI.

'The Iraq crisis was not so much a 'wake-up call' or an isolated mishap, but the logical conclusion of a historic process. The links across the ocean were built at a time when both sides faced a common enemy. They would have survived the disappearance of this enemy, provided both sides shared a similar approach to international crises. But they can no longer be maintained at a time when the US has different strategic priorities, and a radically different perspective on new threats. The future lies in ad hoc arrangements across the Atlantic, ephemeral affairs in which Europeans will always play second-fiddle. It is ironic that the two continents who otherwise know each other so well, ultimately needed Saddam Hussein to expose this stark reality.'

Europe and the United States are no strangers to transatlantic spats; in one way or another, these have happened in every single decade since the end of the Second World War. On each occasion, the dispute appeared acute, and even intractable; weighty commentaries were published predicting the supposed death of the transatlantic link, and the emergence of a new global security order. The dispute over Nikita Khruschev's Soviet disarmament proposals in the 1950s (which entailed the theoretical prospect of the mutual dismantlement of the Warsaw Pact and NATO), the Cuban missile crisis and NATO's internal reform in the 1960s, the sharp differences over the process of Détente in the 1970s, the missile debates in the 1980s, and the huge rows over policy in the Balkans during the last decade are merely some of these examples. Yet each one of these conflicts was ultimately overcome, either through compromise, or by the simple onward march of international events, which often rendered the initial cause of the particular dispute irrelevant.

Seen from this perspective, the current spat over Iraq does not appear to be that important. True, the Cold War – that essential glue which kept Europe and North America together – was missing this time. But the Cold War dissipated by the time Europe and the US locked horns over policy in the Balkans during the 1990s, and these difficulties were ultimately forgotten, paving the way to joint action in Bosnia in 1995 and, more spectacularly, in Kosovo four years later. Furthermore, it is easy to construct an argument that Iraq was the exception, rather than a harbinger of rows to come across the Atlantic. Military operations in Iraq were never covered by the formal mutual defence guarantees which tie the European continent to America; the fact that some Europeans refused to support Washington's policies in Iraq may be regrettable, but it is hardly remarkable. For, after all, Europeans have often objected – and strenuously – to America's policies around the world. Furthermore, the Middle East has been for years one region of the world where the interests of the Europeans and the Americans did not coincide, and where disputes have been ranging for decades. With this Iraq episode now largely out of the way, the optimists will argue that the transatlantic link remains strong, and it will surely survive. Perhaps, but there are serious grounds for believing that the break this time is of a more permanent nature, and that the bad blood generated by the Iraq dispute will endure for years to come.

Psychological Differences
When stripped of its diplomatic noise and histrionics, the transatlantic debate revealed a profound difference in psychology. A welter of opinion polls released over the last few months indicate that Europeans and Americans still broadly share the same aspirations and preoccupations. Reassuring, but hardly very relevant, for on strategic issues, at least, the two continents are moving apart, and fast. The causes of these differences run deep, but can be largely attributed to the different historic experience on the two sides of the Atlantic since the Second World War. For the US, the last six decades were a time of a steady rise from great power to superpower status and, ultimately, to the position of the world's only superpower. In Europe, at the same time, the experience was of a slow, steady decline of the continent's Second World War victors, coupled with the slow but hesitant rise of the countries defeated in that world conflagration. America's problem was very often how to restrain its growing power, how to combine the use of diplomacy with the use of force;

Europe's problem was often how to pool its diminishing power, and how to use diplomacy in order to avoid making any choice about the use of force. These differences are, of course, well-known. Indeed, they are so well-known that both sides of the Atlantic ultimately forgot the profound consequences created by such a different historic experience.

Living in close proximity in relatively small, vulnerable countries, the Europeans have grown accustomed to believing that managing, rather than eliminating security risks is their main preoccupation. There is no doubt that the strategy has worked, at least on the European continent, where a military confrontation is now unthinkable. But the result was a frame of mind that puts a huge premium on creating elaborate processes of conflict avoidance and resolution, and very often on diplomatic form rather than substance. For decades, various structures were created on the European continent, in the full knowledge that they were devoid of any consequence, but in the hope that, one day, they may acquire some significance. The European Union, at least in its infancy, was precisely such a construction. The human rights provisions signed with the Soviet bloc during the 1970s were another example. The fact that the hope was ultimately fulfilled, and that empty constructs suddenly acquired a life of their own persuaded many Europeans that this example can be copied around the world. Coupled with this, there was another persistent European strategy: that of fervently denying even the existence of national interests as the main motor of their states' behaviour, and the determined attempt to assign essential prerogatives of their nation-states to international or regional institutions. The result was a collection of European nations that instinctively believe in the power of diplomacy at all costs, recoil at any show of patriotism, pretend that they no longer espouse national interests and are often fatalistically resigned to the idea that some international crises simply do not have any solution.

It goes without saying that the experience of the US was in precisely the opposite direction. For a country like the US, the idea that national interests must be downplayed is simply absurd. So is the idea that, somehow, international institutions are an absolute necessity. To be sure, most of the US political elite understands that organizations such as the United Nations do have their uses. But, unlike small or medium-sized powers, the US has never believed that the advantages that can be derived from such institutions require serious sacrifices. For a country like the US, international institutions are a luxury, which sometimes can be indulged, but often can also be cast aside. No US politician has ever accepted the idea that managing a crisis is preferable to eliminating it. Few US politicians have been prepared to accept that some crises – and especially those regarded by American public opinion as essential for US security – defy any solution.

Vulnerabilities are not to be managed, but must be eliminated; hence the total 'war against terrorism' or the Weapons of Mass Destruction. And patriotism is to be displayed on one's sleeve, rather than hidden with shame, as most Europeans currently believe. And there is another difference between the two sides of the Atlantic, which is just as important: that of public participation in the formulation of security policies. Both sides of the Atlantic are, of course, democracies. Yet public participation in the formulation of these policies varies greatly. The entire European Union construction was often accomplished despite, and not because of support from the people of the 'old' continent. The political class in Europe instinctively believes that one should not ask their nations too many questions about such matters, because the answers may not be too palatable. The British parliament, that 'mother' of parliaments, has few powers on war-making, and even fewer when it comes to the ratification of international treaties imposing serious military obligations. And in most of the European countries, the use of referenda or formal consultation on foreign policy is actively discouraged. The American public is, of course, not exactly engaged in a serious debate about foreign and security policy either. But the entire formulation of foreign and security policy priorities is much more open to debate – even if the debate often takes place among a restricted circle of people inside Washington. And, when it comes to critical security issues, the opinion of the American public is decisive. The result is very often an American policy which is couched both in very populist, simplistic terms – the need to export 'democracy' or 'justice', for instance – coupled with a search for instant, miraculous solutions.

To be sure, these differences have been apparent for some time; they were the real reason for the string of misunderstandings between Europe and the US during the Yugoslav civil wars of the 1990s. But they blew into the open immediately after the terrorist attacks on the US on 11 September 2001. To a large extent, the assertion that the differences over

Iraq can be traced back to the terrorist attacks on New York may seem strange: after all, the immediate aftermath of these terrorist deeds was also the time when Europe and the US drew closer together, and when even the *Le Monde* daily newspaper in Paris, that mouth-piece of Europe's atavistic anti-Americanism, proclaimed that 'we are all Americans'. But there is little reason to doubt that, just when Europe and America stood united in that fateful September, the seeds of the current serious transatlantic dispute were actually planted.

For many decades, ordinary Americans believed in their territorial invincibility. Apart from Soviet nuclear missiles – now quietly rusting away – few other nations on earth could hit at continental US and fewer still had any cause to do so. Wars happened in other countries, and US governments sometimes had to decide whether to become involved in them or not. The choice, however, was always Washington's, and usually on its own terms. This American myth died in the rubble of the twin towers in New York two years ago: the threat of sudden death at the hands of enemies is now part of the American psyche. And the fact that destruction can come suddenly, perpetrated by people difficult to identify and seemingly impervious to reason, is now accepted as fact by every ordinary American citizen. No serious US politician actually believed that the 'war against terrorism' could be won overnight. And, despite the fashionable criticism from Europe, quite a few American leaders understood that the fight against international terrorism must combine political measures to alleviate the causes of the grievances with the outright use of force against terrorist hubs. But this was hardly the point, for no US leader could publicly advocate the use of diplomacy at the expense of the use of force immediately after the New York tragedy. More importantly, those in the US who suggested that, despite the end of the Cold War, America was more rather than less vulnerable to attacks appeared vindicated. Europe swung behind the US with genuine sympathy and compassion after 11 September. But few in Europe understood just how much the world had changed, and what a profound impact the terrorist attacks had not only on the US psyche, but also on the internal balance of power between hard-liners and moderates inside the Bush Administration. Lending America a hand in the war in Afghanistan and tightening anti-terrorist procedures around the world was considered by the Europeans as a sufficient response. But few European capitals realized that, at least as far as

Washington was concerned, this was the beginning rather than the end of the road.

US and British Propaganda Failures

This is not to say that the US – and Britain, its close ally – are not guilty of fairly serious errors of judgment in presenting their case for a war against Iraq. For, when all is said and done, the entire propaganda campaign surrounding Iraq has been a failure. Seldom before have these two governments – which are otherwise among the slickest of media handlers – stumbled so badly.

On the face of it, persuading international public opinion that a military action against Iraq was necessary should have been easy. Saddam Hussein was, after all, hardly a popular international figure. Indeed, most of those who opposed the war also acknowledged that his removal from power would have been desirable. All of Iraq's immediate neighbours considered him a menace. The elimination of weapons of mass destruction can also be a popular slogan, worldwide. And, despite occasional hiccups, the US has enjoyed higher levels of support around the world since the terrorist attacks of 11 September. But the result?

Almost without exception, overwhelming majorities in each nation around the world were against the war. And, at least in some countries, President Bush was viewed as just as big a problem as Saddam Hussein. The reasons for these failures remain complex. Yet some of the major errors which Washington and London have committed in trying to explain their case against Iraq are relatively easy to pinpoint.

The first layer of difficulties pertains to any US action, wherever it takes place. And, in dealing with Middle Eastern issues, the US has an even bigger disadvantage. Most Arabs regard American policy as duplicitous and hostile to their interests. America's unstinting support for Israel – and seeming indifference to the plight of the Palestinians – is also overwhelmingly resented throughout the wider Muslim world. As the only superpower, the US also automatically acquires the image of bully, however justified Washington may be in pursuing any given policy. Most of the world views the US with a mixture of admiration and apprehension, and often in equal measures. A tinge of instinctive anti-Americanism therefore lingers around the world. America's penchant to justify any action in often subjective but invariably sanctimonious terms such as 'democracy' or the 'common good' does not help either. In short, any attempt by the US to push a new policy is bound to encounter handicaps, however good Washington may be in explaining its thinking.

But this does not mean that such obstacles cannot be overcome. Suspicions about America's policies in the Middle East could have been addressed by combining military pressure against Iraq with political pressure on Israel to return to the negotiating table. This, after all, is what many of America's allies have long suggested. However, President Bush chose to ignore this advice; for much of the Iraqi crisis, he remained silent on the Palestinian-Israeli dispute. The US has now finally revealed its future peace plan for the Middle East, after the initial military victory in Iraq. But, at least as far as international public opinion is concerned, it remains a classic example of doing too little, too late.

Latent anti-Americanism around the world, and the image of the US as a bully, could have also been addressed by patiently trying to build a coalition of countries against Iraq. It is now a well-known secret that preparations for the war against Iraq started more than a year ago in Washington. But for many months, the Administration stubbornly refused to discuss the crisis, either with its close allies or in the United Nations. The delay was fatal, for it deprived the US of the moral high ground and virtually precluded the creation of a solid pro-American coalition. Many countries – particularly in Europe – could have been privately persuaded on the merits of the American case, if this was made gently and persistently. Such an opportunity existed at the NATO summit in November 2002. But for a variety of reasons – some more valid than others – little was said at that stage. The result was that quite a number of European countries were politically unable to accept Washington's line after this was declared publicly, with little international consultation.

Yet probably the biggest public relations mistake which Washington and London committed was to constantly change the official justification for the war. It is now usually forgotten that America's first position was to accuse Iraq of harbouring Al-Qa'ida terrorists. No evidence was ever produced, and this argument faded away, with little explanation. Washington then quickly shifted to claiming that it wanted 'regime change' in Iraq. When some of America's allies – and particularly the British who had some influence – privately pointed out that this was hardly a justification under international law, the argument shifted to weapons of mass destruction. And, as international opposition grew, all three arguments were suddenly blended together: Saddam had to be removed because if he remained in power he would develop terrible weapons, as well as attracting future terrorists. And, yes, in-between there were various claims that the war would bring democracy to Iraq. As every first-year student of public relations knows, the cardinal rule in any successful propaganda campaign is to decide on one simple message, and to stick with it all the way. This is precisely what Washington did not do.

Deep down, there were two other important mistakes. The US failed to realize that it was engaged in the most difficult exercise of all: that of persuading public opinion of the need to resort to war against a supposed danger which has existed for decades, but which has not materialized. At no point did the Americans manage to explain the urgency of their task: as the French have repeatedly asked in the Security Council, if Saddam Hussein was allowed to exist for years, why the urgency of tackling him today? And, even if tackle we must, why does it have to happen immediately? Washington could have provided answers to these questions from the start, but didn't.

The second error which could have been avoided was to realize that the international electronic media has now slipped away from the control of the US and Britain. Even as late as a few years ago, two satellite news television stations – CNN and BBC World – had a pre-eminent role in putting the viewpoint of their home countries to the world. Today, many more international satellite stations fight for this market in local languages, and particularly in the Arab world. The emergence of Al Jazeera as an international television network of influence in the Arab-speaking world startled everyone during the Afghanistan war of 2001. Barely a year later, there were many more entrants into this field; the images beamed by Abu Dhabi television, for instance, during the Iraq war were even more pervasive and powerful. This required a different media strategy; the old technique of holding daily press conferences in the Pentagon or the White House, and expecting these to be beamed around the world in their entirety had outlived its usefulness. American and British politicians duly tried to appear on other media networks. But their language handicaps and their inability to tailor their message to much smaller yet more specific audiences was palpable. The proliferation of satellite news networks has eliminated the advantage that these leaders enjoyed in the past.

None of these considerations prevented the war from starting. But they made the management of the diplomacy before the war much more difficult for both Washington and London. The Iraq crisis should become a classic textbook case of how not to organize an international propaganda campaign. If there is any mistake which could have been made, the US and Britain have committed them in the past few months.

France and Germany

The emergence of France as America's chief international opponent should not have been a surprise: after all, distrust of the United States and its policies is deeply ingrained in the entire French political class, and pin-pricking the Americans has long been elevated to a form of art in Paris. However, even by the standards of their historically rocky relationship, the dispute between France and the US over Iraq remains extraordinary, and it surprised even the most seasoned French observers. In retrospect, however, French opposition, and its intensity, should have been entirely predictable. And the explanation hardly lies in Iraq *per se*.

From the moment President Bush decided to focus on Iraq, he instinctively knew that he could expect trouble from Paris. But the US Administration believed that this would be confined to mere diplomatic noises – the usual kind of official baiting which the French love so much – to be followed immediately thereafter by acquiescence with US policies. After all, this was the behaviour of the French during the first Iraq war a decade ago, when Paris started by criticizing the Americans, only to end up with committing French troops to the fighting, alongside the Americans. So, when the US Administration started drafting its plans for the Iraq war, the assumption in Washington was that the opposition of Russia would be more difficult to overcome, while that of France was still regarded as just a temporary nuisance. Yet what the Americans failed to realize is that France found itself in a unique set of circumstances, which virtually propelled the country to its current position.

President Jacques Chirac has only recently won another full term in office, in a decisive vote. True, the election was won by default, and merely because extreme nationalists divided the left-wing opposition. Nevertheless, Chirac's victory was complete, and crushing. The parties which support him also enjoy a huge majority in the French parliament. The opposition is almost non-existent, and most of the French government consists of Chirac's handpicked appointees. The last leader to enjoy such an unlimited power in modern history was Charles de Gaulle, the president who founded the fifth French Republic more than four decades ago, the leader who first articulated France's anti-American stance and the man with whom Chirac likes best to be compared.

But there was another factor, which helped Chirac into making his decision: Germany. France has long dictated events in Europe through an alliance with its mighty German neighbour. Nevertheless, there was one issue on which the French and the Germans never agreed: relations with the US. While the French had a vision of Europe as a world power counterbalancing the US, the Germans remained steadfast American supporters. All this changed in the last few months. In a desperate effort to retain power, Chancellor Gerhard Schröder of Germany played on opposition to the war in Iraq during his country's electoral campaign. The tactic worked, but only at the price of creating a severe strain in US-German relations. As seen from Paris, this was a historic opportunity which could not be missed: a French president in the unique position of enjoying total power, coupled with a German government which, for the first time since the end of the Second World War, was prepared to support an anti-American policy, albeit on one issue, Iraq. The French knew all along that Germany would not subscribe to any other anti-American excesses. But Chirac also knew that he had a free hand to expand the dispute with Washington from just over Iraq to a question of grander principles, and his German counterpart had no chance of restraining Paris' hand. To make matters even better from the French perspective, Russia's influence over the Iraq question was minimal; President Putin vacillated between wishing to support the Americans and appeasing the anti-American sentiments in Moscow. The result was an impotent Germany wedded to France over the question of Iraq, and a Russia which was ultimately also tied to the French position.

The fierce attitude which France has adopted is therefore entirely explicable. So is the price that Chirac was willing to pay in order to see the policy through. There is no question that Chirac was fully aware of the risks he was taking. But he persisted, because he believed that the potential benefit remained huge: a France which leads all those willing to stand up to American 'arrogance' around the world. With the benefit of hindsight, it is now clear that no amount of British or US concessions in the

UN Security Council would have made the slightest bit of difference to France's position over Iraq. For Iraq was never Chirac's main aim; his gambit to control Europe's relations with the US was the main objective. And this required the paralysis of the UN Security Council, as well as the damage that NATO sustained over its attempt to provide assistance to one of its members, Turkey. At every stage, Chirac refused any compromise and upped the stakes even further. The idea that, somehow, there was a median line between the position of the US and that of France is almost certainly fanciful; a combination of factors made the rift almost inevitable.

So, has the French position succeeded? For a while, the French did most of the running and retained the initiative. There is little doubt that US plans in the Middle East have been greatly complicated by France's position, and that Chirac himself has reaped personal benefits. His popularity remains sky-high not only at home, but in some other countries as well, and particularly throughout the Middle East. In many respects, President Chirac has managed to steal the mantle of Russia as Europe's chief US opponent. But he has clearly over-reached himself in Europe, at almost every level.

First, the way the French leader hijacked the question of Iraq annoyed Germany, its chief ally, and put a severe strain on Franco-German relations. Chancellor Schröder has probably gone too far now to admit publicly that he was wrong over Iraq. But there is no doubt that the first task of any future German government after the disappearance of Schröder would be to repair relations with Washington, and that this would be accomplished by distancing Berlin's policies from Paris. Chirac may still appear the leader in the Franco-German alliance for the moment, but this is unlikely to last after the next German general elections, which may well take place within a year. France has failed to tie Germany permanently to an anti-American agenda. To make matters worse, France has also managed to infuriate other key European countries, such as Italy or Spain. For many years if not decades, the rest of the members of the European Union got used to the fact that, whether they liked it or not, they had to accept the Franco-German axis on their continent. The link between France and Germany was too strong to oppose publicly, and the dangers of doing so were too great, compared to the potential advantages. But the French behaviour over Iraq propelled other medium-sized European countries to act: for the first time, they were prepared to stand up to the Franco-German alliance, and did so vigorously. A psychological threshold has been passed in Europe, and this will have major consequences on the future conduct of policies within the EU for years to come.

Just as important, moreover, was the question of France's attitude towards the former communist countries of Eastern Europe. Overall, the nations of Eastern Europe have reacted to the crisis in Iraq in very similar terms to the rest of their brethren on the continent. Every opinion poll conducted in the former communist east indicated large majorities against the Iraq war, and a high degree of cynicism about America's real motives in the Middle East. The difference, however, was that this cynicism about the war has not been translated into a mass protest movement. Politicians in the east were, therefore, under less pressure from their electorates, and remained determined to support the United States, almost regardless of the consequences. The reasons for this sharply different reaction were partly based on history, and partly on cool strategic calculations. The soon-to become European Union member states from the continent's east feel that they still owe a debt of gratitude to the US for helping with their liberation from communist dictatorship. Washington may have never been ready to fight the Soviet empire in order to liberate Eastern Europe, but the US was first to support them after the Soviet Union collapsed, and NATO was the first institution to admit them as full members, well before the EU decided on its own enlargement. Baiting the Americans may be a French sport and, increasingly, a German occupation as well, but this strategy remains a taboo in all the East European states, without an exception. Coupled with this, there are colder strategic considerations as well. The emergence of a new Franco-German axis in Europe, an axis which this time is explicitly directed against US policies, is regarded with deep dismay in all the East European states. After all, France and Germany were also the two major European countries that were quite content to leave Eastern Europe under Soviet occupation for decades; French flirting with the Soviet Union and Germany's accommodation with Soviet dictators is not forgotten in the East. Nor are the East Europeans persuaded by the French and German argument that the United Nations should be the ultimate arbiter in any future crisis; the idea that Russia, their old colonial master, could ever be in a position to veto

American actions remains anathema in every former communist state. In short, the East Europeans did not necessarily support the war in Iraq, but they were determined to cling to the United States because the alternatives were much worse. If the French and Germans understood what was going on, they would have tried to listen to the East Europeans, and dispel their fears. But they did nothing of the kind: furious that the small East Europeans even dared to be different, they brushed their complaints aside, and proceeded to do as they wished. France and Germany's opponents in Europe did better, by harvesting this East European frustration. When the British, Spanish and Italian leaders decided to sign their open letter of support for the US in the Iraq crisis, they duly enlisted a few signatures from key East European countries. The fury of Germany and France knew no bounds, and diplomats from the two countries spent nights trying to persuade East European leaders to repudiate the British-Spanish-Italian initiative. Paris and Berlin failed; the public letter of support for the US was ultimately endorsed by every East European country. One would have thought that, after this stinging public rebuke from the 'new' Europe, the French and the Germans would have got the point. Far from it: undeterred, Paris and Berlin upped the diplomatic stakes. In an act of supreme folly, Turkey's decision to invoke Article 4 of the North Atlantic Treaty by demanding consultation within NATO was initially blocked by France, Germany and Belgium. For the East Europeans, this was probably the gravest of all actions. As seen from Eastern Europe, Article 4 of the North Atlantic Treaty is just as important as the famed Article 5, containing the mutual security guarantee. None of the East European members of the Alliance have Western forces permanently stationed on their territory. They therefore put great store on the understanding that, should they ever be threatened, the Alliance would come to their aid. If countries within the Alliance suddenly decide to interpret the provisions for emergency consultations in times of crises according to their own wishes – as has initially happened over the Turkish request for consultations – this is tantamount to saying that the Eastern Europeans cannot be sure of an automatic security guarantee. But this was not all that the French and the Germans decided to do. Undeterred, they proceeded to engage in highly-visible negotiations with Russia's President Vladimir Putin over Iraq; the sight of the Russian leader in Paris and Berlin amounted to the final red rag for the East Europeans. In essence, the French did not simply ignore the worries of the Easterners; they did everything possible to infuriate them. All told, France and Germany have forfeited a great deal of influence in Eastern Europe, and it will take Paris and Berlin years to redeem their reputation in that region. The European Union which will come into being after 2004 will be much closer to the vision of Britain and, indeed, of the US, than to that of France.

US Defense Secretary Donald Rumsfeld's dismissal of Germany and France as 'old Europe' may have been both undiplomatic and simplistic, but it stung Paris and Berlin because it was fundamentally true. But this does not mean – as Washington evidently hopes – that the transatlantic debate will subside when the EU and NATO enlarge their composition by admitting new members. The former communist countries are relatively poor and small. Since they cannot afford to constantly annoy France or Germany, their preferred policy will be to keep silent, while their bigger continental brethren fire off verbal missiles across the Atlantic. The difference, however, is that both Washington and the bigger European states will periodically force them to clarify their position and make a choice. During the last year alone, 'new' Europe was forced to opt for either Europe or the US not only over Iraq, but also over Washington's stance on the International Criminal Court. And, when Romania chose to openly support the US position over the Court's jurisdiction, it was immediately castigated as 'non-European'. In essence, precisely what everyone continues to deny appears to be happening – the test of belonging to 'Europe' is now seen to entail an almost automatic rejection of the US position. This is almost guaranteed to make any future dispute between the US and Europe both difficult to manage and more acute.

The Future? More of the Same!

Even as late as a decade ago, the occasional absence of a transatlantic consensus was invariably regarded as a major diplomatic failure. Today, however, transatlantic unanimity on any major international issue is routinely portrayed in Europe as a 'humiliation', yet another supposed indication of Europe's inability to 'grow up' or, to use another favoured cliché, 'stand on its own feet'. The latest row about Iraq was not so much a dispute across the Atlantic, but an internal debate between individual European governments about their attitudes towards the US. The characterization of the British Prime Minister as America's 'poodle' – initially promoted by the British media but then picked up, *sotto voce*, by key European politicians – apparently required no substantiation: it was self-evident from the very fact that Tony Blair refused to publicly criticize the US. Conversely, the claims of French or German leaders to represent Europe's 'true' feelings on Iraq were also never substantiated, for they were allegedly proven by the simple act of opposition to what the US wanted to do. The howls of anger which greeted the publication of a letter from eight European leaders supporting the US position on Iraq were instructive. There was little criticism of what these leaders actually said; instead, the wrath was directed at the very idea that some Europeans had the temerity to disagree with their continental partners, and side instead with Washington. The conclusion is inescapable – the old habit of transatlantic partnership has now been replaced by an instinct of differentiation: the idea that the natural and even desirable state of affairs is for the Europeans to disagree with the Americans, but, ideally, to articulate this disagreement in unison.

But the most tragic backdrop to these otherwise irrelevant diplomatic shenanigans is the growing military gap between Europe and the US. The gap is widening because of two simultaneous trends: the refusal of some key Europeans – notably Germany – to invest in their defence and the staggering growth in the US defence budget. To be sure, Britain and France have increased their military spending in order to retain long-range expeditionary warfare capabilities. The efforts of smaller European countries also deserve an honourable mention. But the reality remains that, apart from some niche European capabilities, the US military does not need the Europeans for any military operation. The Europeans remain politically useful, partly because no Washington administration wishes to be seen to be fighting on its own, and partly because the image of the US as a leader of a 'coalition' reassures the American public that they continue to fight in the service of humanity. Curiously, therefore, a growing sense of American unilateralism goes hand in hand with an increased desire for coalition-building.

But, as the Iraq crisis indicated, there are important limits to the coalitions that the Americans are still interested in creating. First, because the US does not need any major military capabilities, neither the total number nor the firepower of the coalition members matters much. A relatively substantial military power like Britain could therefore be coupled with a string of otherwise militarily irrelevant countries in any configuration, just to make up numbers. Secondly, because the Pentagon generals often regard such countries as a nuisance, the US is not usually prepared to pay a high political price for their membership in a coalition; Washington does not demand much, but is not offering much either. And, finally, the coalition itself can change, according to the crisis or the political calculations; the make-up of the group is relatively unimportant, as long as it allows the US president to announce the start of hostilities, leaning against a backdrop of colourful flags from many nations. This is not merely a transitory phenomenon. The lessons which the Americans drew from the Kosovo war is that they will never again put themselves in the position of supplying most of the military assets, but listen to advice about how to conduct a war from countries whose territory is often smaller than one US training camp. This was evident in Afghanistan when the US politely thanked NATO for its expressions of solidarity, but told the Alliance to stand aside. During the latest Iraq crisis the Americans wanted to do better, by creating a niche role for NATO, mainly in the protection of countries close to Iraq, such as Turkey. But this effort met with resistance inside the Alliance itself, a rebuff that no US military planner is likely to forget .

Paradoxically – given the current tone of the transatlantic debate – the immediate aftermath of the Iraqi conflagration is still likely to give both Europe and the US plenty of opportunities to patch up relations. But even then, the lull in the dispute will be relatively short: sooner or later, allegations will emerge about the involvement of some European companies in sanction-busting trade with Iraq during Saddam Hussein's rule, and these will sour the mood yet again. Nor is Washington likely to forget the real significance of its recent transatlantic tussle. Germany – Europe's biggest single power – will remain the continent's beached whale, a vast, militarily flabby lump, increasingly alienated from the US, unable to tackle its economic problems and with a feeble government to boot. France will retain its tactic of pin-pricking the Americans. The smaller former communist countries in Europe will continue to fret about such disputes, but will be unable to influence them. And Britain will persist in trying to act as a new transatlantic bridge, earning the brickbats of many other Europeans for its efforts. Meanwhile, the US will increasingly regard the Europeans as an amorphous mass of rich but limp-wristed states, who may be picked one by one or in groups in order to make up 'coalitions', provided the US leadership in any war is guaranteed, and only if the political price demanded for this coalition is not too onerous.

The Iraq crisis was not so much a 'wake-up call' or an isolated mishap, but the logical conclusion of a historic process. The links across the ocean were built at a time when both sides faced a common enemy. They would have survived the disappearance of this enemy, provided both sides shared a similar approach to international crises. But they can no longer be maintained at a time when the US has different strategic priorities and a radically different perspective on new threats. The future lies in *ad hoc* arrangements across the Atlantic, ephemeral affairs in which Europeans will always play second-fiddle. It is ironic that the two continents, who otherwise know each other so well, ultimately needed Saddam Hussein to expose this stark reality.

12. Between Peace and War
Iraq in Perspective

Douglas Hurd

Lord Hurd was Foreign Secretary during the 1991 Gulf War. His remarks are taken from a speech given at RUSI on 27 January 2003.

'A genuinely democratic Iraq might well act as a fresh spur. But everything would depend on the circumstances. At one end of the range of possibilities a new Iraqi government installed by British and American military force and sustained by our occupying troops for months or years after a war in which many Iraqis were killed, could have the opposite effect. The reaction against what would appear as imperialism rather than liberation could be destructive. We might win the war in six days, and then lose it in six months.'

Disarming Saddam

The decision between peace and war facing our government in the next few weeks is a new one; that is to say it does not flow inexorably from decisions already taken. Many of us have accepted the argument put particularly by the Foreign Secretary that the best way of ensuring, without war, that Iraq is finally deprived of weapons of mass destruction is to pile up the pressures on Saddam Hussein, including the deployment of weaponry and troops.

But it cannot follow that because weapons and troops are now being deployed we are bound to go to war. We are not in 1914, when according to some critics it was their earlier decision to mobilize that forced the Kaiser and the Tsar to declare war. No considerations of face could prevent President Bush and our Prime Minister from accepting a climb down by Saddam Hussein to comply with UN demands or a peaceful coup in Iraq resulting in his exile. Such an outcome would certainly be best for the world and for Iraq. No military timetable should compel war when a successful outcome, namely a disarmed Iraq, may be feasible without war, for example by allowing more time to the UN inspectors.

It seems likely that Saddam Hussein, as well as being an odious dictator, has again sought to deceive us – that is, that he possesses chemical and biological weapons and has been groping for nuclear. We have faced such deceit from dictators before. I remember the day when President Yeltsin told me in the Kremlin how his predecessors had deceived us in precisely this field.

The United States successfully led us in a policy of combined deterrence and diplomacy in dealing with the threat from the Soviet Union. It is following the same policy today in dealing with North Korea. President Kim of North Korea knows that he and his colleagues would be obliterated within hours of using against us any of the Weapons of Mass Destruction which he possesses. In dealing with the smaller though still real threat from Saddam Hussein, the United States is inclined to abandon deterrence and go for pre-emptive strike. There seems to be two reasons for this. First, such a strike is more certain if one of its results – the risk that deterrence might not work – is removed. Second, Saddam Hussein is weaker militarily than either the Soviet Union or North Korea. It is hard to dispute this discrimination as a calculation of reality – but also hard to put it in any consistent moral context.

Before a final decision is taken to send in our servicemen to kill and be killed, several questions need to be considered, of which I name two.

Security in the Middle East

The first concerns the Middle East as a whole. Would it be a safer and better place after a successful attack to overthrow Saddam Hussein? I do not myself doubt that military success would come quickly. Loyalty to the dictator would be a rare commodity once the missiles began to fly.

Neither the Iraqi people, nor other Arab governments nor indeed Islamic fundamentalists have any reason to admire or trust Saddam Hussein. He has failed to establish himself, as Nasser once did, as the accepted leader of Arab nationalism throughout the region. Furthermore, we have an interest in doing anything we reasonably can from outside to further democracy in the Middle East. The democratic deficit in the region holds back the healthy growth of a stable civil society. I believe that Egypt in its own way, the Palestinians when they are given a chance and others will before long, move towards greater democracy. Some smaller states – Qatar, Kuwait and Bahrain – have taken their own initiatives already. A genuinely democratic Iraq might well act as a fresh spur. But everything would depend on the circumstances. At one end of the range of possibilities a new Iraqi government installed by British and American military force and sustained by our occupying troops for months or years after a war in which many Iraqis were killed, could have the opposite effect. The reaction against what would appear as imperialism rather than liberation could be destructive. We might win the war in six days, and then lose it in six months.

The risk would be increased because of the most serious mistake the Americans have yet made. They have put on hold any sustained and insistent initiative towards an even-handed peace between Israel and the Palestinians. The mistake is not yet irretrievable. But so far they have swallowed whole Mr Sharon's argument that Israel is a straightforward ally against terrorism, and ignored his policies of oppression and settlement which inevitably breed new violence. They have made their own and our task in the Middle East more doubtful and dangerous. Conditions in the West Bank and Gaza are appalling, as every Arab viewer of television now knows. We run the risk of being seen not as liberators but as protectors of an oppressor.

Security in the West

This leads to the second question: what is the effect on our own safety? It was essentially for self-defence that we went to war in Afghanistan and would go to war in Iraq. We freed the Afghan people from the Taliban, but after Bali, Mombasa and the alarms which sound around us every day, who can say that he or she feels safer now than before the Afghan campaign? We kicked the hornets' nest to pieces, and the hornets buzz more angrily around us. It seems certain that we are now faced with a ruthless long-lasting struggle against growing numbers of Muslim fundamentalists and extreme nationalists through Asia and North Africa who do not hesitate to use violence against the West. For them murder is an aim in itself. It is not clear what connection exists between those who shot at American soldiers and civilians in Kuwait, those who murdered Baptist missionaries in Yemen, and whoever stabbed a British police officer in Manchester. Whether there is a pyramid of terrorist authority called Al-Qa'ida or, more likely, a loose network of different groups with similar ideas, is relatively immaterial: these are our enemies. Do we help or hinder this essential struggle against terrorism by attacking Iraq? Do we increase or diminish the numbers and determination of those enemies? Would we thus turn the Middle East into a set of friendly democratic capitalist societies ready to make peace with Israel, or into a region of sullen humiliation, a fertile and almost inexhaustible recruiting ground for further terrorists for whom Britain is a main target?

Conclusion

The outcome would probably lie somewhere in-between, neither wholly good or bad. The scales are evenly balanced and I do not envy the British Cabinet in its decision. The test is not one of virility, but of wisdom. You will see from the way I phrase the questions that I am inclined to pessimism about the answers. I may be wrong in that, but not I think in putting the questions. In our modern democracy the government needs not a unanimous but a general support for war before it orders our forces to fight.

There are some who will always be opposed, as they were in the Gulf War in 1991. There are many others, in all political parties and none, who supported that war of straightforward liberation but who this time are doubtful. These are strong supporters of NATO, the Anglo-American alliance and our armed forces. If a decision is made to commit our forces to war, such people (including myself) will shut up and hope that we were wrong. But the issues are cloudier than in 1991, and the awkward questions not always answered. There is still time and need for the government to listen and respond.

October 2002, RUSI Journal, Vol. 147, No. 5

13. High Noon for British Grand Strategy

Michael Codner

Michael Codner is Director of Military Sciences, RUSI.

'We cannot assume that Iraqi people anywhere will see the forces of an invading and occupying coalition as liberators. Consent, assent or even acquiescence may not be established early, if ever. It will not be possible to configure occupying forces at an early stage for constabulary roles. Indeed, it may be necessary to replace combatant nations' forces with forces of nations that might be considered to be benign before stabilization can begin properly.'

If

'We must ensure that he does not get to use the weapons he has, or get hold of the weapons he wants'. These are the words with which Tony Blair, the British Prime Minister, ended his introduction to the dossier, *Iraq's Weapons of Mass Destruction: The Assessment of the British Government*, presented to the public and Parliament on 24 September 2002. That was also your correspondent's deadline and it would be a favour if these jottings were read in the context of the moment at which they were written. History is rarely as kind to statesmen.

This statement of purpose by Tony Blair is pretty precise and unequivocal. If the United Nations inspectors are not able to carry out their task unhindered – if Saddam Hussein will not assent to the supervised destruction of the subject weapons and the capacity to generate them, as discovered by inspectors and intelligence; and if no guarantee can be put in place that Iraq could not subsequently create weapons of mass destruction and the means of their delivery – then 'we' must use other ways and means. 'We' in this context are the international community but the rhetoric implies that the United States, to whose 'demands' the British Government has offered 'support', and the United Kingdom will be the champions in this cause.

A great deal has been said and written in recent months about the morality and legality of military ways and means against Iraq and indeed the diplomatic processes towards international assent or acquiescence. This article gives no view on these matters except insofar as they shape combat in a possible war. It is rather a brief discussion of practical military options and implications for a UK contribution in what might be a lonely coalition with the US.

Coercive Diplomacy and the Onset of Violence

It bears mention that military force is already being used in this present crisis. There is of course the on-going air enforcement of the No Fly Zones by the US and UK. One might also consider Operation *Desert Fox*, the denial operation that followed the failure and withdrawal of the United Nations inspectors in 1998 as a step in the process of disarming Saddam Hussein. More immediately, however, the US is using military forces to support its coercive diplomacy. It has the military capability to attack Iraq and, probably, to remove the present regime. It has stated its very clear intention to use force for these purposes. It has begun a build-up of forces in theatre. Compellence does not begin when violence is actually used. It starts when there is a subject of coercive action (Iraq) and a believable threat of organized violence by the coercer (the US at this stage).Whether or not some of the Bush Administration believe that violence is the only way to solve the Saddam problem, to create this perception is precisely the technically (as opposed to morally or legally) correct way to apply strategic coercion effectively.

Fortune of War

Of course the four-and-a-half-year strategic pause since *Desert Fox* belies any true sense of a crisis provoked by Iraq. Maybe 'line in the sand' is a more apt metaphor than 'cliff edge' for the present situation. It is a construction based cumulatively on what Saddam has not done, what he might very well be doing, and indeed his continuation as an actor and factor that is providing the sense of immediacy, rather than any decisive action or event on Iraq's behalf.

This distinction is not trivial. The sort of war that might follow should be defined in part by the urgency of any danger and the seriousness of the threat, directly or indirectly, to national interests. A third factor is the risk associated with the endeavour and the probability of success. Clausewitz's dictum that war is the pursuit of policy by other means is frequently cited. Rarely mentioned is his warning that commitment to war will set in train a course of events whose outcome is unpredictable. He therefore presents a paradox to those who would apply cost-benefit analysis in terms of well-being to the decision to go to war. The risk of military failure can be mitigated by using a vast superiority in capability so effectively that military success is not in any real doubt. A nation may be disarmed. Territory may be occupied or re-occupied. A regime may be removed. There would still be huge risk in translating this achievement into political ends and in the political, social and environmental consequences, not least if the venture is widely perceived as having breached legal or moral principles.

Legality and Utility

So for present purposes, there are perhaps three sorts of war. There is a war of overwhelming necessity in the face of a clear and present danger. There is a war to defend a principle that is essential for international order. And there is an intervention of choice designed to make the world on balance a safer and better place or to prevent it from becoming less so. The primary military objective of the first is to remove the immediate danger. It may well be a leap into the dark and cost-benefit considerations will be set aside in the first instance. Legality will probably be a matter of mutual or collective self-defence and issues of the right of pre-emption and proportionality would be for later. In the second, it is to right the wrong in which case the legality of the operation is all-important as an action of questionable legality would be self-defeating. Cost-benefit considerations would probably be futile as they would take the form of a comparison of a quantity of suffering in the short term set against the universal benefit of an enduring principle. However, there is a question of utility in the longer term if regional or world order is severely damaged. In the third, the need for the benefit to exceed the cost is of the essence. Intervening nations would of course want to ensure that their actions were legal, notwithstanding some mooting about terminating humanitarian crisis versus national sovereignty.

On the basis of this analysis the evidence from the dossier points to this third sort of war. But neither the US nor the UK government have characterized any future commitment to combat as an elective intervention. Earlier rhetoric from the Bush Administration, with its scant regard for due process by the United Nations, suggested a war of overwhelming necessity. The modified position that seems most closely to match the view of the British Government is that it would be a war of principle about the authority of the United Nations, whether or not it can be persuaded to exercise it. In either case chaos downstream of the initial military outcome would be a secondary consideration. As for the conduct of military operations, however, a war of the second sort would entail an interpretation of the principle of proportionality that the majority of the international community would perceive to be appropriate, in particular governments who might have covertly acquiesced to war and those who abstained 'constructively' from dissent. World opinion will be very sensitive to excessive collateral injury. In any event, numbers of civilian deaths will be large unless Iraq collapses at the first onslaught. And it will not be possible for a US-led coalition to treat the post-combat situation in Iraq and the region as someone else's problem, whatever the US subsequently chooses to do.

Coercion in War?

So how might a possible campaign unfold? Importantly, the war will essentially be one of denial in the technical sense. It will be necessary to eliminate capability, in particular Weapons of Mass Destruction and the means to achieve these, but also the means by which the regime exercises control. The regime itself must either be destroyed or so constrained and modified in its behaviour that the pattern of events after Desert Storm is not repeated. A US-led coalition would not be attempting to coerce Saddam Hussein into abandoning his previous ways. A compellent campaign of the Kosovo sort would be totally inappropriate except insofar that a preliminary air campaign of denial would prepare the battlespace for insertion of ground forces. Incremental air attack on strategic targets for chiefly coercive effect would do more to unite the population around the regime and habituate it to increasing suffering. There may of course be a coercive effect of a denial campaign. However, the target would not be Saddam but the perceptions of Iraqi military and paramilitary forces, the population as a whole and, perhaps, those close to the centre of the regime who might be convinced that the struggle is hopeless and that a deal could be struck without Saddam.

Denial of Capability

The target sets for preparatory air attacks would not be unlike those for Operation *Desert Shield* in 1990–91. The priority would be Iraqi air defences, the Weapons of Mass Destruction and associated capabilities, the strategic command and control arrangements of the regime, and operational command and control of forces. If intelligence provided Saddam himself as a target early in the operation, that would be a bonus and would assume the highest priority. Attack on conventional military and paramilitary capability would follow, beginning with elite forces both human and equipment. Attack on conscript forces should focus on equipment.

It would be important that air systems including cruise missiles should be gathered in large numbers in advance so that the initial raids could be on as wide a scale as possible and give the impression of a cataclysm. The most humane outcome to the war would be a collapse of national military power and national will to continue, and this will not be achieved by incremental attacks. It is likely that the highest priority targets will be arranged to be in centres of population. Civilian casualties are likely to be very high in the early stages of the war with the prospect of far fewer innocent deaths later on.

The initial air denial campaign will be accompanied by special forces operations to gather intelligence of potential critical targets and to conduct reconnaissance and target acquisition for air strikes. Special and specialist forces may also carry out specific denial operations chiefly against weapons of mass destruction and strategic command and control.

Needless to say, intelligence will not be sufficient at the outset to identify all weapons of mass destruction capability or strategic command and control, some of which will be mobile or able to redeploy rapidly. A systematic hunt to locate and attack both will need to continue throughout the campaign and will be an important element of major ground operations.

Major Ground Operations

Although an early collapse is a possibility, it would be essential to plan on the assumption that remaining military, paramilitary and guerrilla forces will resist any ground invasion of Iraqi soil. The obvious entry point for a large ground invasion would in the first instance be through Kuwait.

However, it is unlikely that the ground campaign would involve systematic control of territory advancing on a broad front from the south through Baghdad to the north. It is more likely that centres of military control and local government will be seized at an early stage to complete the isolation of the Iraqi leadership. These would provide some early focus for stabilization of regions that could declare themselves autonomous or invite in assistance from neighbouring powers that could be hinder the post-combat settlement.

It would be very important, nonetheless, to have committed and prepared from the start of any air campaign sufficient ground forces to occupy the entire country. It would be irresponsible not to be able to establish military government in the event of a collapse of the Iraqi regime and any formal or informal surrender. It may be that Turkey and Jordan would allow the passage of post-combat stabilization forces, and subsequent logistic support, across their borders. They may be prepared (covertly) to make host-nation support arrangements to this end. It is unlikely but not inconceivable that the US would deal with Iran similarly. In any event, Iran would need to be managed as it was during the overthrow of the Taliban in Afghanistan to prevent an unwanted invasion by Iran of southern Iraq on the pretext of stabilization.

Nuclear Coercion

It is most unlikely that the threat of chemical or biological response by Iraq will be eliminated early in the air campaign. These weapons could threaten occupying forces and could be used against Israel or forward-deployed forces outside Iraq. During the 1991 Gulf War, then US Defence Secretary Dick Cheney made a veiled threat of nuclear retaliation to any such use. Since then both the US and British governments have in policy statements alluded more or less directly to the 'sub-strategic' use of nuclear weapons in retaliation to chemical and biological attack. It will be extremely difficult for any coalition to present nuclear deterrence as one of the planks of its strategy, particularly as objectives of regime change may render Saddam Hussein personally invulnerable to coercion and prepared to seek, in the words of Fred Ikle, 'transcendental objectives'.

Regime Change

It is essential to this plan that the regime would be isolated and thereby relieved of its power either to conduct military operations or to govern the country. If in the process Saddam and other key individuals are killed, the process will be much simpler. However, a possible scenario might be the disappearance of Saddam at an early stage and a request from remaining elements of the regime to negotiate a termination of combat operations. There would be strong international pressure to bring hostilities to an end and an interim government – doubtless closely supervised by the US - might be a means to early stabilization. It is unlikely, however, that the US would provide any guarantees for the survival of a compliant Ba'athist regime. No doubt a new constitution and early elections would be preconditions of any negotiations.

Asymmetric Response

Governments associated directly or indirectly with an attack on Iraq would need to prepare for asymmetric attack against their own homelands and information infrastructure. One suspects that Saddam would not, at least in the early stages of a war, be able to call on much loyalty beyond Iraq. Things could change, however, if the war was protracted, involving large numbers of civilian deaths, which would allow time for resentment to build up in the Arab world.

Military Government and Stabilization

If much civilian infrastructure is destroyed during the war and if local and regional governments do not exist or cannot be trusted by occupying forces, there may be the need for a period of direct military government. Indeed, this would be a moral (and probably legal) responsibility of occupying forces. They would need the support of large numbers of civil affairs staffs and preparations would need to be in place in advance for civil police to be available. Unlike IFOR in Bosnia, the occupying forces would not be able to distance themselves from aspects of civil administration and law enforcement. Full military government should only be a temporary state and should be maintained for as short a period as possible. However, there may be a need to ensure that civil administration set up to assume responsibilities is not infected by supporters of the previous regime. The experience drawn from the former Yugoslavia is not of the same order. For all the war crimes in that theatre, the perpetrators have not been demonized to the extent that the Iraqi regime has been characterized as innately evil. During the occupations that followed the Second World War the process of 'epuration', of eliminating Nazis and Fascists from positions of influence or authority, was one of the impediments to the transfer to civilian government. The Allied experiences of occupation in Germany, Austria, Italy and elsewhere - now largely forgotten - bear review today.

In the same context, we cannot assume that Iraqi people anywhere will see the forces of an invading and occupying coalition as liberators. Consent, assent or even acquiescence may not be established early, if ever. It will not be possible to configure occupying forces at an early stage for constabulary roles. Indeed, it may be necessary to replace combatant nations' forces with forces of nations that might be considered to be benign before stabilization can begin properly.

The Longer Term

This brief account of a possible campaign might appear to be unduly ghoulish and pessimistic. In its military operation, however, the US will not accept any significant risk of failure and will plan for the worst case. Its allies – whoever they will be – will need to so the same. As for the post-combat phases, the US will clearly want a co-operative Iraq to emerge. Washington will also seek an Iraq able to look after its oil and with an appropriate share of the balance of power in the Gulf, which could stand the test of, say, a collapse of the Saudi regime. As many critics of war in Iraq have pointed out, the problems will lie in the post-combat tasks of occupation, stabilization and normalization. It is outside the scope of this article to comment on the wider security situation after a war.

The United Kingdom's Part

Your correspondent is not alone in his view that one of successive British governments' highest-level grand strategic objectives is to enhance the security of the UK by influencing the execution of US security strategy. This objective is not formally stated in public documents, nor perhaps is, in such a crude formulation, a part of the consciousness of government. This influence is usually discreet but sometimes, as over the past twelve months, overt. Influence is a matter of gaining and preserving confidence. One might aver that it is based not only on diplomatic support and an intellectual contribution, but also on having the capability to give significant military support. British military capability needs to be more than a token if there is to be influence over American military strategy. It needs to be needed.

The US is unlikely, though, to sustain any capability shortcomings of its own once it has found that it has a dependency on the UK. The British contribution must be needed for its behavioural contribution. It may be possible, for instance, for British forces to take risks under certain circumstances that would be politically unacceptable to the US. And UK forces may have certain qualities stemming from differences in doctrine that are alien to the US way of war.

If we assume that the Prime Minister will take Britain into this war, it follows that the British contribution should be where it is most needed, where British forces can behave most usefully. It may be that the United Kingdom will commit armour and mechanized infantry for bulk that may, for once, be needed and air systems for long-range attack in order to have some influence over strategic targeting. A carrier and amphibious shipping will contribute to offshore basing where there is not much host nation support. And sub-strategic Trident will allow us to share nobly in the awkward and unpopular business of nuclear deterrence of chemical and biological attack.

However, there are two broad types of operation in which British capability might be needed rather than nice to have. The first is in the various operations using special forces and specialist forces described earlier. The second is in providing the framework headquarters and significant forces for the process of stabilization. No surprise, perhaps. In this respect, if in no other, the Afghanistan case study is illuminating.

High Noon

The Prime Minister played a unique role in harnessing world sympathy for the US in the wake of 11 September and in the subsequent coalition building. Britain has been shackled by history to the US over the business of Iraq. Even if that were not the case, however, our grand strategy dictates that we should be on the inside modifying US policy where we have a common interest. We have the prospect now of a very big war, requiring huge numbers of ground forces, and a shortage of allies. Military success in combat operations is likely, although there could be large numbers of casualties. It is the mess afterwards that could well be our particular challenge, however. Alarmingly, the newly-released National Security Strategy of the United States is rife with the language of isolationism and going it alone. Will we be safely on the inside or on the way out?

End Note

Ghost Stories

John A. Nagl

Lieutenant Colonel John A. Nagl commands the 1st (US) Battalion, 34th Armor at Fort Riley, Kansas. He served as the operations officer of Task Force Centurion in Al-Anbar in 2003 and 2004, where the task force lost twenty-two soldiers Killed in Action and was awarded more than one hundred Purple Hearts and a Valorous Unit Award.

It is Hallowe'en as I write this, and I am being visited by ghosts, friendly little ghosts who go away when I give them a piece of candy.

It is Hallowe'en as I read this, and I am being visited by ghosts, some friendly, some not, whom I have kept away, locked inside me for years, but Brian Turner, Ghost One-Three Alpha, that son of a bitch, he is calling them back.

I have put them away, kept them inside, the ghosts of the lieutenants and the Captain and the First Sergeant, their bodies torn by shrapnel or a sniper's bullet or gone, just gone, into hundreds of shreds of flesh the size of my still-living hand, but Ghost One-Three Alpha speaks to ghosts, he calls to his ghosts, and they bring mine along for company, and now they will not go away.

If you have been to war – if you have held a microphone in your hand, begging for MEDEVAC with the blood of your friends on your hands, pouring out your soul over the airwaves to keep your friends from becoming ghosts, from joining the shades in an unholy company of men who have given limbs and eyes and hearts – if you have held that bloody hand mike, then Ghost One-Three Alpha will take you back to that day, that day when time stopped and life stopped and never really started again, no matter how hard you try to make the ghosts go away.

Here, bullet. Here. Take me, so that I can join the ghosts, so that my company will again be complete, armless, legless, eyeless, a company of memories, a company of shades.

We will again visit the land of the Two Rivers, where the Tigris and the Euphrates meet, where the elephant grass grows man-high in the irrigation canals. We will return to the warren of Baghdad streets, where the women wail and the children beg, and Ghost One-Three Alpha will call commands and Apache Red One will take point and Bulldog Six will grin again, that wonderful grin he had, full of joy, back when he still had a face.

We will join the company of ghosts who were our enemies, who waited for us in alleys and in canals, who wore sandals and man-dresses and spoke in a language we could not understand and fought for reasons we could not understand but they fought well, these men we turned to ghosts, they fought us and we fought them and now we are all together, what is left of us, in the half-light shadows that Sergeant Turner weaves together, calling ghosts, ghosts that will no longer leave me.

This article is a response to Here, Bullet, *a collection of poems by Brian Turner (call sign Ghost One-Three Alpha).*